Hawthorne's Literature for Children

D1543551

>>>>>> **LAURA LAFFRADO** <<<<<<

HAWTHORNE'S LITERATURE FOR CHILDREN

The University of Georgia Press   ⟨✤⟩   *Athens and London*

© 1992 by the University of Georgia Press
Athens, Georgia 30602
All rights reserved

Designed by Erin Kirk
Set in Berkeley Oldstyle Medium
by Tseng Information Systems, Inc.
Printed and bound by Braun-Brumfield, Inc.

The paper in this book meets the guidelines for
permanence and durability of the Committee on
Production Guidelines for Book Longevity of the
Council on Library Resources.

Printed in the United States of America

96 95 94 93 92   C   5 4 3 2 1

Library of Congress Cataloging in Publication Data

Laffrado, Laura.
Hawthorne's literature for children / Laura Laffrado.
p.   cm.
Includes bibliographical references and index.
ISBN 0-8203-1417-X (alk. paper)
1. Hawthorne, Nathaniel, 1804–1864—Criticism and
interpretation.   2. Children's stories, American—History
and criticism.   I. Title.
PS1892.C46L34   1992
813'.3—dc20   91-28002
                                                  CIP

British Library Cataloging in Publication Data available

Versions of the author's readings of individual Hawthorne
works ("Queen Christina" and "The Gorgon's Head")
previously appeared in *Children's Literature*
and *Nathaniel Hawthorne Review*.

For Phil

CONTENTS

⟫⟫⟫⟫⟫ ACKNOWLEDGMENTS ⟪⟪⟪⟪⟪

Many people have offered their support and encouragement in the course of this project. I am grateful to Robert Daly, whose high standards and generosity guided my graduate studies and helped shape my professional life. I am also indebted to Kenneth Dauber, whose critical insight and example helped me pursue and develop my ideas. Beth Kalikoff and Hans Ostrom, my colleagues at the University of Puget Sound, provided generous readings and good advice. In other significant ways, this project has benefited from the help and support of Diane Christian, Bruce Jackson, and Lea Bertani Newman. The University of Puget Sound offered generous financial assistance in the final stages of the project. Shelley S. Bott gave me valuable assistance in preparing this manuscript for publication.

Additionally, I am indebted to my professors at Vassar College and the State University of New York at Buffalo for the intelligence and devotion which filled their classes and turned my head.

I owe thanks to my sister, Kathy, and her husband, Peter, who for years have given me invaluable support when it meant the most to me. I also owe thanks to my mother and father, who provided a childhood full of books and an unshakable faith in education.

Finally, I am most grateful to my husband, Phil, to whom this book is dedicated, for everything.

Nathaniel Hawthorne's reputation as the author of six children's books was once celebrated but is now virtually forgotten. All his children's books were collections: *Grandfather's Chair, Famous Old People*, and *Liberty Tree* (1841) were historical stories; *Biographical Stories for Children* (1842) contained biographical sketches; and *A Wonder Book* (1851) and *Tanglewood Tales* (1853) retold classic myths.

Before he wrote these books, Hawthorne had at various times considered joining the popular movement toward writing for children. Several factors influenced the men and women who, in increasing numbers, were turning to children's literature. Some welcomed and wished to perpetuate the mid-nineteenth century "emergence of a special literature designed for the younger generation" (Crandall 3).[1] Most of this popular juvenile writing was heavy-handed and moralistic, part of "an impressive campaign of informal indoctrination of young Americans" (Crandall 3). Others were inspired by what Alison Lurie, in discussing the history of children's literature, has called "the value put on childhood by writers like Blake and Wordsworth, which suggested to men and women of genius that writing for and about children was a serious and worthy occupation" (xii). For all, there was the prospect of financial gain.

Before Hawthorne published his first collection in 1841, he had had several earlier experiences with writing for children. His sentimental sketch "Little Annie's Ramble" appeared in the annual *Youth's Keepsake* in 1835 (Pearce 287–288).[2] The following year Hawthorne provided "'two folios'" for *Peter Parley's Universal History* (Pearce 289), a series of juvenile books published by Samuel Goodrich. In "compiling"

(Goodrich's term) the piece, Hawthorne followed Goodrich's instructions, using Royal Robbins's *The World Displayed, in Its History and Geography* (Pearce 289). Hawthorne was offered one hundred dollars for the job ("poor compensation" [*Letters* 15: 247]), and, when asked to put together another installment for three hundred dollars, he refused (Mellow 74). Though Hawthorne considered it hackwork, the Parley series introduced him to the possibility of writing a lengthier work for children.[3]

Months later, after receiving an enthusiastic letter from Longfellow, to whom he had sent a copy of the recently published *Twice-Told Tales*, Hawthorne wrote in reply, "I see little prospect but that I must scribble for a living. But this troubles me much less than you would suppose. I can turn my pen to all sorts of drudgery, such as children's books &c" (*Letters* 15: 252). As he renewed his acquaintance with Longfellow, a former college classmate, Hawthorne seems to have thought of him more and more in connection with children's literature.

In 1838, he again approached the subject, this time in the form of a proposed collaboration with Longfellow, a work to be called *Boy's Wonder Horn*. Hawthorne's yearlong enthusiasm for the project outpaced Longfellow's. In a March 1838 letter to Longfellow, Hawthorne wrote, "Possibly we may make a great hit, and entirely revolutionize the whole system of juvenile literature" (*Letters* 15: 266). Again, in October 1838, he wrote, "I suppose it would require only a short time to complete the volume, if we were to set about it in good earnest" (*Letters* 15: 276). And, finally, in January 1839, when he realized Longfellow's enthusiasm did not match his own, he promised, "Really I do mean to turn my attention to writing for children. . . . It appears to me that there is a very fair chance of profit" (*Letters* 15: 288). Longfellow never returned to the idea, but Hawthorne, a year later, began *Grandfather's Chair*.

Hawthorne's correspondence with Longfellow on this subject articulates his primary purposes in turning to children's literature: to revolutionize a system that he thought encouraged poor writing and false truths; to write quickly and well, publish, and aim for success; and to make money. Further, in his March 1838 letter, the correspondence is used to form his thoughts on how a book for children could be effectively structured: "Ought there not to be a slender thread of story running through the book, as a connecting medium for the other stories?" (*Letters* 15: 266). This was the narrative structure he would use in his six children's books, the same one employed in the earlier but abandoned collection of short stories, *The Story Teller*. Longfellow's authority and established reputation had already prompted Hawthorne to send him *Twice-Told Tales* in hopes of Longfellow's writing a favorable review. He did so, publishing in the *North American Review* "a lengthy review . . . full of generous praise" (Mellow 79). Their proposed collaboration must have encouraged Hawthorne to use the correspondence to discover Longfellow's thoughts on writing successfully and to develop his own thoughts on writing for children.

Later, the various narrators Hawthorne created in his children's books continued to reflect his concern with status and authority. In *Grandfather's Chair, Famous Old People, Liberty Tree*, and *Biographical Stories*, Hawthorne (the unmarried, childless, financially unsuccessful author) is juxtaposed with Grandfather (rich in experience, descendants, and history) and with Mr. Temple (rich in success, paternity, and morality). In *A Wonder Book*, Hawthorne, by then himself rich in marriage, paternity, and vocation (and thus older, more established, and confident in his authority), creates Eustace Bright, an undergraduate at Williams College and an aspiring and slightly foolish writer. Eustace Bright returns briefly in the introduction to *Tanglewood Tales*, but an older and more experienced Hawthorne, who had seen too much of the world's misery, deals with him briefly and skeptically questions his innocent view of that collection's myths. Hawthorne's narrators change in response to Hawthorne's perception of his cultural position: when he has little cultural authority, he creates the pious, patriarchal Mr. Temple; when he is financially successful, a happy father, and a well-known author, he creates (and affectionately patronizes) the foolish Eustace Bright.

These changes of narrator are joined by changes in subject matter, framing devices, and Hawthorne's own self-image. In my reading of these works, Hawthorne is attempting to establish a certain mode of discourse, a way in which he can write confidently. This discourse is dependent on his happiness, book sales, and mastery of the artistic space that the children's books allow him to explore. This artistic exploration and the events of his life directly affected the writing of the children's books. The initial discovery of the neutral territory when writing *Grandfather's Chair, Famous Old People*, and *Liberty Tree*; the rejection of that territory when mired in discontent while writing *Biographical Stories*; the golden age of his life, personally and artistically, in *A Wonder Book*; and, finally, the newly probed limits of his childhood audience, difficulties with recounting thrice-told tales, and the grim events of his life in writing *Tanglewood Tales*: all map the course of Hawthorne's personal and artistic lives, his lives in the worlds of the actual and the imaginary.

The artistic space and mode of discourse involved in the children's books result in differences between Hawthorne's psychological insights into childhood in his children's books and those in his other fictions. In the children's books, Hawthorne repeatedly shows children as innocent, sensitive, and empathetic. They fully experience whatever they encounter. They deeply engage narratives, especially on an emotional level. Their experience is readily shaped because of their receptivity. These qualities are not, however, invested with the sentimental pieties of Victorian treatment of children, which often led to the children being killed and thus consecrated. It is not the death of the child but the pollution of the child that the adult world must fear. The adult world needs to consider how it educates its children, lest their experience be unwittingly vitiated.

Hawthorne's psychological insights into childhood in his other fictions, especially *The Scarlet Letter* and "The Gentle Boy," initially correspond with those in the children's books. Pearl repeatedly wonders about Dimmesdale's emotions and actions, attempting to read him into her experience. Pearl is the symbol of Hester's sin, and Pearl's joy, grief, dancing, and mischief show that, in her unconscious empathy, she has absorbed the emotional resonance of the letter. Like Pearl, Ilbrahim in "The Gentle Boy" responds emotionally and fully to his influences. In each scene, he locates himself next to whatever emotion dominates. His father's grave is "'under this heap of earth, and here is my home'" (*Twice-Told Tales* 72). Both children are deeply and immediately shaped by their experiences precisely because they are children. In their natural empathy, they become what happens to them. That other children torment them is equally revealing. Those children, too, have been shaped by their experiences—in both cases, the ignorance and prejudice of their parents and community.

In the children's books, however, Hawthorne repeatedly stresses narrative as a strategy to shape children's experiences and thus to control their education. For Hawthorne, children are exquisitely receptive to their experience, and the adult world carelessly underestimates the effect of its opinions and actions on children. Narration is shown to be a strategy that can protect, nurture, and properly educate children. Grandfather, Mr. Temple, Eustace, and Hawthorne, in his preface to each collection of stories, all express varying degrees of awareness that stories are involved in a world of power, are written or told for certain interests against other interests. In the children's books, more so than in his other fictions, Hawthorne stresses the power of narratives—historical, biographical, mythical—to mediate the experience of childhood.

In Hawthorne's conception of children's literature, that narrative power is extended to the artist, or Hawthorne himself. Writing for children allowed him freedom of artistic exploration—freedom to tell truths about history, experience, and faith, about the dangers to innocence in a rationalistic and materialistic world. An examination of these writings colors current critical understandings of the trajectory of Hawthorne's literary career and allows for a reenvisioning of that trajectory, a reenvisioning of that life.

CHAPTER ONE

The Transcendence of Temporality:
The Whole History of Grandfather's Chair

I n 1840, Hawthorne wrote a series of three short children's books about American history: *Grandfather's Chair, Famous Old People,* and *Liberty Tree.* They were published the following year. A decade later, after the success of *The Scarlet Letter,* they were reissued, along with *Biographical Stories for Children,* in *True Stories from History and Biography*; the three historical works were then titled *The Whole History of Grandfather's Chair.*

Because Hawthorne engages American history in his other fictions, his rewriting of history for children has been compared with his rewriting of history for adults. Most recently, Nina Baym and Michael Colacurcio have included the histories in their examinations of Hawthorne's writing and the role of moral history in the early tales.

Aside from examining the use of history, however, the critical literature on Hawthorne's fictions continues to neglect *The Whole History.* Calvin Earl Schorer's "Juvenile Literature of Nathaniel Hawthorne," an unpublished dissertation (1949), treats the subject most completely. But little has been added in recent decades.[1] The children's histories still have much to offer readers of Hawthorne. In these histories, Hawthorne first located and acquainted himself with a reality where the real and fabulous are conflated. The very writing of his children's books thus enabled him to distance himself from his own daily reality and personal history.

In *Grandfather's Chair, Famous Old People*, and *Liberty Tree*, Hawthorne related events of American history for children, using tales told by Grandfather and framed by the fireside reactions of Laurence, Clara, Charley, and Alice, his grandchildren.

In the brief preface to *Grandfather's Chair*, Hawthorne stresses the historical "truth" of these stories: "Setting aside Grandfather and his auditors, and excepting the adventures of the chair, which form the machinery of the work, nothing in the ensuing pages can be termed fictitious. The author, it is true, has sometimes assumed the license of filling up the outline of history with details, for which he has none but imaginative authority, but which, he hopes, do not violate nor give a false coloring to the truth" (6). In Hawthorne's terms, therefore, a nonfictional treatment of history can be a "true" one. His logocentric assumption that there ever can be one reading of history responds to the inaccuracies and deliberate distortions in nationalistic histories of the time. Yet the "American" history in these works will be Massachusetts history; and the stories told will be chosen to stress certain views of history and experience. Consequently, while Hawthorne disdains historical lies in all his fictions, here he remains (perhaps unconsciously) well within the ideological project of nineteenth-century Whig New England.

The children's histories Hawthorne wrote thus borrow from both of the nineteenth-century schools of thought on children's literature. Though the histories are not the overtly nationalistic propaganda seen in popular juvenile literature of the time, they nonetheless mirror their political culture. At the same time, Hawthorne's artistry associates the books with the romantic emphasis on childhood and writing for children.

In each book, Hawthorne creates alternate worlds that are metaphors for the real one. His use of imagination, symbolized by magic and alchemy, allows his characters (and thus the writer) to travel through space and time, to be somewhere else. In writing these histories, Hawthorne distanced himself from his personal history, from the Boston Custom House, and from his wearisome bachelorhood. A full decade before he climbed to the upper floor of the Salem Custom House and found that "the floor of our familiar room has become a neutral territory, somewhere between the real world and fairy-land, where the Actual and the Imaginary may meet, and each imbue itself with the nature of the other" (*Scarlet Letter* 36), Hawthorne managed to escape his everyday life in his children's books.

Aiming his writing toward a different and less elitist audience allowed Hawthorne to construct worlds of escape for his young audience and for himself. On the surface, *Grandfather's Chair, Famous Old People*, and *Liberty Tree* are history retold for the young. Beneath the surface, all three texts repeatedly present alternative realities, worlds of magic, alchemy, and disguise, that encourage an escape from the hegemony within and without the stories. For auditors, readers, and author, the stories ultimately transcend the boundaries of time.

Grandfather's Chair

In all three books, Grandfather's chair guides readers to the lost personal worlds of historical figures: "It causes us to feel at once, that these characters of history had a private and familiar existence, and were not wholly contained within that cold array of outward action, which we are compelled to receive as the adequate representation of their lives. If this impression can be given, much is accomplished" (5–6). The chair serves as a vehicle to the "private and familiar existence," a recurring image in Hawthorne's fiction, to another time and another sensibility. The outward action that usually constitutes historical representation displaces the personal world and the power and meaning located in the familiar. Because of the chair, historical significance will mix with the personal, the actual with the imaginary.

The early pages of the book signal the movement away from "that cold array of outward action." The frame device of the first sketch begins with a "pleasant afternoon," "little Alice," who comes "fluttering like a butterfly into the room," and the observation that "a summer afternoon is like a long lifetime to the young" (9).[2] This dreamy childhood scene is an alternative reality, the lost paradise of childhood, to be entered when one has wearied of the old world. Even before Grandfather tells his first tale, then, the boundaries of time have begun to blur: an afternoon can be a lifetime; paradise can be regained in the imagination.

In "The Lady Arbella," the first story in *Grandfather's Chair*, transport into the world of the actual results in sadness, fragility, and death. The fairly grim text supports the fears Hawthorne had confessed in his preface: "The author's greatest doubt is, whether he has succeeded in writing a book which will be readable by the class for whom he intends it. To make a lively and entertaining narrative for children, with such unmalleable material as is presented by the sombre, stern, and rigid characteristics of the Puritans and their descendants, is quite as difficult an attempt, as to manufacture delicate playthings out of the granite rocks on which New England is founded" (6).

For Hawthorne, writing American history for the young creates a tension between what he sees as the required lively narration and the "unmalleable material" of American history itself. To write American history for children successfully, then, requires a literary alchemist, one who can make the untractable material of history malleable. The material can then be fashioned into or adapted to a new form. In Hawthorne's children's books, the demands of American history (in *A Wonder Book* and *Tanglewood Tales*, classic myth) and the demands of the genre (children's literature) conflict, and he negotiates the conflict with varying degrees of success.

From the moment she leaves for America, Lady Arbella is caught between worlds. Her past, England, becomes for her a dreamworld that she will never see again. Since she looks "too pale and feeble to endure the hardships of the wilderness" (15), it is evident that she will not survive her New World of hardships where people variously clear, hew, hoe, drag, shout, dig, snatch, and run, while Lady Arbella "watches" (16). This robust world of active verbs is the world of the actual, where Lady Arbella cannot thrive.

In Lady Arbella's America, the sensitive cannot survive. The New World defeats, not only the sensitive woman, but also, by extrapolation, the sensitive person, since Mr. Johnson, Lady Arbella's husband, dies "'at Boston within a month after the death of his wife'" (19). Years later, in *The Marble Faun*, Hawthorne explores this territory in a larger and more personal fashion, developing it into an exploration of the American artist's survival in America and in the world. In *Grandfather's Chair*, the idea manifests itself as a warning from Grandfather (surely a character who could not now survive the transatlantic journey) to the equally weak children: those who leave their dreamworlds behind are doomed to one world and one reality. The unmediated world of the actual leaves the sensitive only a sad and fragile existence that leads to death.

In "The Red Cross," as in "The Lady Arbella," the change from Old World to New World is again complicated by the effects of otherness. The story briefly illustrates John Endicott's destruction of the banner of the Red Cross, the "national banner of England, under which her soldiers . . . fought for hundreds of years" (22). The banner featured a cross "'abhorred by the Puritans, because they considered it a relic of Popish idolatry'" (22). Once a symbol to inspire the sacrifice of a nation's blood, the banner is now read by Endicott as obsolete and heretical. A national symbol becomes an offensive rag; the world and its signs have changed dramatically, nearly magically.

Boundaries of old and new, permissible and lawless, conflict: "'As the clergy had great influence in temporal concerns, the minister and magistrate would talk over the occurrences of the day, and consult how the people might be governed according to Scriptural laws'" (22). Secular and spiritual law meet and form the official power structure. John Endicott must negotiate the secular and the spiritual, just as Lady Arbella negotiated two worlds.

The salient differences between the two tales (one features a dying woman, the other a robust man; one a new world, the other a more established world; one resignation, the other defiance) reflect the problematics of alterity. One's epistemology will determine which world is actual, which imaginary, and which one merits one's deepest faith and allegiance.

The vibrant world of "The Pine Tree Shillings" more successfully and happily conflates two worlds. The strongbox overflowing with pine tree shillings, the bride "round and plump as a pudding," the eccentric father with his "plum colored coat" (37) and buttons made of shillings, the weighing of the daughter balanced by her weight in shillings, all are qualities of a different time and genre, a time as remote from the actual as it is from the "private and familiar existence." There is so much money in the story that it cannot be viewed as real money, so much bride that she becomes larger than life.

The enlarged and distorted symbols of commercial success (money, clothing, overeating) prohibit this story from revealing the private existences of its historical figures. Yet we are also far beyond the coldly related action of "The Red Cross." "The Pine Tree Shillings" takes place in the past perfect, a time that requires imagination since it never existed. Names and articles of reality fuse its existence with the existence of the actual past. While Lady Arbella languished in a new world that we recognized as old, "The Pine Tree Shillings" offers an old world that is always newly imagined. This conflation of the actual and the imaginary will become characteristic of Hawthorne's artistic discourse, the way in which he will write most confidently. "The Pine Tree Shillings," brief as it is, is the first appearance of this interplay in the children's works.

Captain John Hull, the story's alchemist, turns " 'battered silver cans and tankards, . . . silver buckles, and broken spoons, and silver buttons of worn-out coats, and silver hilts of swords' " into " 'an immense amount of splendid shillings, sixpences, and threepences' " (36). He profits greatly by this ability to turn waste into legal tender: his title, "mintmaster," and his shrewd bargain with the magistrates reveal a power rooted in the classic American quality of commercial ingenuity. Hawthorne sketches Hull briefly, dwelling perhaps too self-consciously on his gleaming and almost magically obtained piles of wealth, such wealth and means being even more remote from the common person in Hawthorne's time than they were in Hull's.

Still, "The Pine Tree Shillings" suggests a world where capitalism and imagination can be yoked together. Hawthorne's stultifying and marginally remunerative employment stands sharply against the pleasures of consumption that result from Hull's wise but seemingly effortless actions. The hyberbolic intensity of the description of Hull's world encourages Hawthorne's escape into that remote and imagined past, just as it reveals his rewriting of the emerging industrialist-capitalist order that made his present life so complexly bound by economic facts. "The Pine Tree Shillings" offers the history of John Hull for children while it edits the mass culture that eventually resulted from such zealous attention to material wealth.

Throughout the collection, Grandfather's admiration authorizes the children to think highly of both character and the character's actions. The impact grows as the collection continues and Grandfather becomes a more opinionated narrator (just as Hawthorne, simultaneously, becomes a more authoritative writer). Though Grandfather relates Hull's story with great relish, he gives greater approval to John Eliot (of whom Grandfather "was a great admirer" [45]) in "The Indian Bible."

As narrator, Grandfather should admire John Eliot, who is shown at the end of his life, attempting to open a correspondence with the world by translating the English Bible into the Indian tongue. Hawthorne's desire to write for a popular market, Grandfather's wish to entertain and educate his grandchildren, and Eliot's hope to open one culture to another all reveal individuals engaged in a series of formal linguistic acts. In Grandfather's description of Eliot's work, for example, the language is "'utterly unlike all other tongues—a language which hitherto had never been learnt, except by the Indians themselves, from their mothers' lips—a language never written, and the strange words of which seemed inexpressible by letters'" (45). In "The Indian Bible" sounds are turned into words, but only by Eliot. Once this is accomplished, only Eliot and the Indians can understand the sounds as words: "'Learned men, who . . . were supposed to possess all the erudition which mankind has hoarded up from age to age'" (46), remain incapable of assembling the sounds into language. Eliot's work involves a world that cannot be read by scholars, one that remains unread outside the community. But due to Eliot, that world is now noticeably outside, visibly unread and inaccessible despite Eliot's desire to communicate it.

Grandfather's Chair repeatedly highlights past worlds that are as unreadable for the common reader as the Indian Bible was for Eliot's colleagues. Like John Eliot, Hawthorne is the only one who can see these worlds well enough to read them for the community. Just as Eliot tries (and ultimately fails) to link Indian and Puritan cultures through language, so Hawthorne tries to link the actual and the imaginary of the past through the language of *Grandfather's Chair*. The picture of Eliot sitting in solitude while translating the Bible into the Indian tongue and so entering a world removed from common language and understanding corresponds with Hawthorne sitting in the Custom House while translating history books into fiction for children and so entering a world isolated from the common reader.

Eliot worried that, were he to fail, his Bible would be left unfinished and his correspondence left unread. Hawthorne forever worried that his correspondence with the world was ultimately unread or misunderstood. Hawthorne, Grandfather, and Eliot all fear that worlds seen and read by them will remain uncommunicated should they fail at their respective tasks. "The Indian Bible," the only story in *Grandfather's Chair* that deals solely with language, reflects the dilemma of the artist striving to communicate what he fears is both essential and ultimately incommunicable.

Like "The Pine Tree Shillings," "The Sunken Treasure" is associated with the fairy tale and points to worlds unseen, objects unread. In its pages William Phips, "'a poor man's son . . . born in the province of Maine'" (57), moves from rags to riches, becoming Sir William Phips, governor of Massachusetts. Phips knows early in life that he will achieve greatness: "'He often told his wife that, some time or other, he should be very rich, and would build a "fair brick house" in the Green Lane of Boston'" (58). Since Phips's prophecy is realized in the story, Grandfather must be sure that the children do not misread these seemingly effortless, fairy-tale gains: "'Do not suppose, children, that he had been to a fortune teller to inquire his destiny. It was his own energy and spirit of enterprise, and his resolution to lead an industrious life, that made him look forward with so much confidence to better days'" (58). Grandfather knows Phips's prediction is the stuff of wishes, not the stuff of reality, and so tries to make Phips's good fortune the result of energy, enterprise, and resolution.

Grandfather's assertion that American enterprise and drive fueled Phips's success is undercut as Phips goes from poverty to wealth, stones turn into money, someone goes crazy at the sight of an inconceivable amount of money, and a shrub leads the way to buried treasure. Just as John Eliot's unintelligible sounds were words, so Phips's stones are silver: "'After a day or two, they lighted on another part of the wreck, where they found a great many bags of silver dollars. But nobody could have guessed that these were money-bags. By remaining so long in the salt-water, they had become covered over with a crust which had the appearance of stone, so that it was necessary to break them in pieces with hammers and axes. When this was done, a stream of silver dollars gushed out upon the deck of the vessel'" (62).

Though the element of alchemy is somewhat mediated by explanatory phrases ("by remaining so long in the salt-water" and "crust which had the appearance of stone"), the language encourages a reading of the process as magical. Hammers and axes release a force so volatile that it emerges, animate, in a "stream" and "gushes" out of its prison. This strangely vitalized, literally powerful fortune gives Phips power and success in his money-oriented culture.

As in "The Pine Tree Shillings," the large amounts of currency that enable one to participate successfully in the competitive forces of culture are achieved in unconventional ways. Neither Hull nor Phips competes in conventional ways for his wealth; neither fortune is modest, hidden, or the product of years of labor. Both Hull and Phips are portrayed as having a natural affinity for money, an ability to read the possibility of money in old belt buckles or crumbling stone. In this revision of the way to wealth, there is no machinery of industrialization, no life of frenzied productivity; no one works long, unpleasant hours, and no one fears an uncertain economic future. The alternative worlds in these stories result in the pleasures of upper-middle-class existence. The young auditors, the readers, and the writer escape confrontations with the harsh machinery of capitalist culture.

In the brief concluding section following "The Sunken Treasure" and ending *Grandfather's Chair*, a paragraph hardly meant for a younger audience defends the fanciful treatment in the stories:

> "But, after all," continued Grandfather, "any other old chair, if it possessed memory, and a hand to write its recollections, could record stranger stories than any that I have told you. From generation to generation, a chair sits familiarly in the midst of human interests, and is witness to the most secret and confidential intercourse, that mortal man

can hold with his fellow. The human heart may best be read in the fireside chair. And as to external events, Grief and Joy keep a continual
vicissitude around it and within it. Now we see the glad face and glowing form of Joy, sitting merrily on the old chair, and throwing a warm,
firelight radiance over all the household. Now, while we thought not of
it, the dark clad mourner, Grief, has stolen into the place of Joy, but not
to retain it long. The imagination can hardly grasp so wide a subject, as
is embraced in the experience of a family chair." (65)

Surely this paragraph is not directed to the audience wooed earlier
with pine tree shillings and sunken treasure. If the experience of the
chair is that of the human heart, then almost all of one's imagination
is demanded to present it accurately. Indeed, because "the imagination
can hardly grasp so wide a subject," the use of fancy is necessary. Once
we emerge from the world of "The Sunken Treasure," imagination re-
cedes, and Hawthorne's discourse returns to the world of the actual,
with its insistence on facts and explanations. Even Grandfather's defense of the fictive use of the chair is couched in the secular and
sentimental language familiar to Hawthorne's adult audience.

But Hawthorne had learned much about the neutral territory that
enabled him to write confidently, and Grandfather's aside defending
excessive imagination is followed by a cat leaping in the window and
settling herself in a chair. " 'Pussy,' said little Alice, . . . 'you look very
wise. Do tell us a story about Grandfather's Chair!' " (67). Alice's request appropriately ends the book. Alice has learned enough in the
course of the stories to approach unconventional sources of knowledge. If stones can turn into silver, chairs into tour guides, and worlds
into dreams, then cats, perhaps, can talk. The stories in the collection have encouraged the children's awareness of narration, history,
time, and truth. Grandfather's arbitrary interpretations do not cancel
this heightened awareness. The possibility of the children's arriving at
conclusions not promoted by Grandfather remains. Who knows what
sort of story Alice will imagine the cat's telling? *Grandfather's Chair*
ends between fact and imagination, with the wise cat ready to begin
its narration.

Famous Old People

In the opening pages of *Famous Old People*, the representations of both Grandfather and Grandfather's chair have much to do with times and places: "But now, in the autumnal twilight, illuminated by the flickering blaze of the wood-fire, they looked at the old chair, and thought that it had never before worn such an interesting aspect. There it stood, in the venerable majesty of more than two hundred years. The light from the hearth quivered upon the flowers and foliage, that were wrought into its oaken back; and the lion's head at the summit, seemed almost to move its jaws and shake its mane" (74). Grandfather, seated in the chair, is "gazing at the red embers, as intently as if his past life were all pictured there, or as if it were a prospect of the future world" (74). Grandfather is seated in the present and thinking of the past or perhaps the future (as if the two were somehow interchangeable). The personified chair inhabits "the shadowy region of the past" (74).

This gliding from past to present to future is watched over by "the wood-fire, . . . a kindly, cheerful, sociable spirit, sympathizing with mankind, and knowing that to create warmth is but one of the good offices which are expected from it. Therefore it dances on the hearth, and laughs broadly through the room, and plays a thousand antics, and throws a joyous glow over all the faces that encircle it" (73). Before the first formal sketch of the book begins, we know the text will be watched over by a benevolent and powerful spirit, the chair is alive and has "never before worn such an interesting aspect," and Grandfather sits, brooding on temporality.

In a discussion of Hawthorne's desire to "embrace the career of literature as historical" (520), Michael Colacurcio examines Hawthorne's belief "in the reality of time" (519) and asks: "For where had one encountered a more flagrant abstraction from time than in America itself? Where, between a spiritualized ancestor worship and a naturalized apocalyptics, had a Party of Irony more plainly cried out for existence? And how could its irony have been other than historical? What it needed to insist on . . . was precisely the full reality of all times and places" (520). In *Famous Old People*, both temporality and, more specifically, "flagrant abstraction[s] from time" attract Grandfather's attention and the chair's presence.

The preface of *Famous Old People* attempts to justify a sequel to *Grandfather's Chair* ("It is therefore sufficiently complete in itself, to make it independent of our preceding volume" [72]), but no such justification is needed. In *Famous Old People*, Grandfather, Grandfather's chair, and the stories themselves are richer in significance than in the first volume. Even Grandfather's position as the collection opens signifies a more complex web of discourses where the boundaries of time have lost their rigidity.

Grandfather finishes the history of Sir William Phips (beginning *Famous Old People* with the subject with which *Grandfather's Chair* ended) and includes a reference to " 'the witchcraft delusion' " (77). He gives "his auditors such details of this melancholy affair, as he thought it fit for them to know" (77). One of these details is that the affair "had originated in the wicked arts of a few children" (77). Since his immediate audience is composed of children (as is Hawthorne's reading audience), Grandfather must see "fit for them to know" their own capacity for evil and for causing " 'a very frightful business' " (77). Later in *Famous Old People* there will be more cause to question Grandfather's narrative purpose, but for now the reference is a glancing one, and the first sketch of the book is introduced.

Since children have the potential to be evil, they need proper training to perform well in life, as "The Old-Fashioned School" illustrates. Schoolmaster Ezekiel Cheever is another alchemist, one who can perform the terrible and powerful trick of turning boys into grown, responsible men. Along with this skill, Master Cheever has the gift of prophecy and can see the futures of his schoolboys: " 'One urchin shall hereafter be a doctor, and administer pills and potions, and stalk gravely through life, perfumed with assafoetida. Another shall wrangle at the bar, and fight his way to wealth and honors, and, in his declining age, shall be a worshipful member of his Majesty's council. A third—and he is the Master's favorite—shall be a worthy successor to the old Puritan ministers, now in their graves; he shall preach with great unction and effect, and leave volumes of sermons, in print and manuscript, for the benefit of future generations' " (83).

In addition to possessing the powers of alchemy and prophecy, Master Cheever manages to escape time: the schoolroom is a timeless place that, year after year, is always full of boys. Outside of the schoolroom, however, away from his base of power, Master Cheever, like Wakefield venturing out into "busy and selfish London," feels "as if his place were lost, and himself a stranger in the world" (85). But Wakefield leaves home and hearth for urban anonymity, while Master Cheever leaves the schoolroom for holiday, not forever, and to "go home to dinner" (85). Only when Master Cheever leaves the timeless for the world of unmediated reality is his power shaken.

Impressive as Master Cheever's powers are, they pale beside Grandfather's. His gift of prophecy includes the ability to see into the past (Master Cheever's schoolroom) and to predict the future, a future already in the past for Grandfather and his grandchildren. In "The Old-Fashioned School," Grandfather constructs a past world where the schoolroom is as real as the world outside it, as real as the schoolboys' futures and Master Cheever's prophecies. Grandfather's blurring of these worlds and times is characteristic of his discourse. Once the children realize the arbitrary nature of the imposed boundaries of time, they have been educated, and they are ready to leave the schoolroom without fearing (as does Master Cheever, who is enslaved by his power) that their place in reality will be lost and that they will be strangers in the world.

"One or two evenings afterwards," Grandfather sits "meditating, as was his custom, about things long past" (86). Hawthorne's employment in the Boston Custom House while writing *Famous Old People*, the multiple meanings he assigned to "custom" in the later "The Custom House," and his lifelong struggles with the dictates of custom in his life and art suggest the highlighted semantic possibilities of Grandfather's custom in *his* life and art. Despite the assertion that Grandfather's meditations are regularly rooted in the past, in *Grandfather's Chair* and *Famous Old People* these meditations mix "things long past" with the present, the future, and the imagination. Grandfather's custom is to bring into the present "things long past" through his meditations and subsequent storytelling. This process of adulteration allows Grandfather the power to transcend time and to insist on the full reality of all times and places in his historical revisions.

It is not surprising, then, that when the " 'procession of the boys of Boston' " comes by, Grandfather wakes "in a sort of amazement, as if he had been asleep for a great many years, and were just awakened by the drums and shouts" (86–87). This echo of Rip van Winkle warns of the dangers associated with stepping outside restrictions of past, present, and future: Grandfather, when he wakes, has momentarily lost his place in the world. He cannot read the signs of the present time. Once Laurence explains the disturbance, Grandfather is relieved ("'Ah, well!' said Grandfather smiling"), and immediately links the present with the past. "'Boys are the same in every generation—always aping their fathers—always taking a mimic interest in grown men's affairs'" (87).

This judgment mediates Grandfather's earlier "amazement" at having lost himself in the stream of time. Now it appears that one who steps outside custom risks becoming only temporarily lost. As every generation shares similar qualities, the Rip van Winkle need only inquire as to, for instance, the cause of the current procession, since all other motives will be timeworn and clear.

Yet some magical possibilities of the unimagined (in the past) but real are beyond custom. At the end of this section, Grandfather is "interrupted by the entrance of three newspapers, which were all published that same evening, and every evening of the year" (90). As he reads, Grandfather's meditations center again on the past but are rooted in the perspective of the present: "Meantime, Grandfather could not help thinking how our forefathers would have wondered, had they foreseen the innumerable host of newspapers that now fly forth, from all quarters and in all directions, throughout the land. What a dull, incurious people must they have been, when one little weekly sheet sufficed for a whole continent!" (91).

Newspaper printing and distribution are beyond the past and so would be seen by "our forefathers" as constituting a magical process wherein suddenly animate newspapers "fly forth" in a "host" like spirits "throughout the land"; the process is outside of our forefathers' custom, and they therefore view it as magical because they cannot read the signs. The labeling of these ancestors as "a dull, incurious people" contradicts the lessons of *Grandfather's Chair* and *Famous Old People*. Were they truly dull and incurious, the printing process would not have evolved and the newspaper would not have become the textual representation of mass culture that it is. Momentarily rooted in the present, Grandfather's musing reveals an inability to imagine New England before industrialization and urbanization brought about a modern society dominated by commerce and mass production.

The chair passes next to Cotton Mather, whose " 'fasts and vigils made him meagre and haggard, and probably caused him to appear as if he hardly belonged to the world' " (94). In "The Rejected Blessing," witchcraft and black magic bar Mather from a place in culture as he studies the smallpox epidemic of the 1720s. By examining African tracts, Mather discovers the possibility of the smallpox inoculation. However, this information is rejected by the populace, because "they recollected how he had led them astray, in the old witchcraft delusion" (102). Even as he walks down the street, women snatch their children away, literally keeping him from future generations.

Local physicians disparage Mather's discovery of a possible cure, because "no such thing as inoculation was mentioned by Galen or Hippocrates, and it was impossible that modern physicians should be wiser than those old sages" (101). By consulting obscure documents, Mather has meddled with time, as is evident by the physicians' and the citizenry's resistance to the inoculation. In "The Rejected Blessing," Mather is clearly ahead of his time. After taking us back to the small-pox epidemic, Grandfather takes us forward to " 'after years, when inoculation was universally practised, and thousands were saved from death by it' " (104). Then the people go back in time and remember " 'old Cotton Mather, then sleeping in his grave' " (104). During Grandfather's sketch, Cotton Mather has been out of time, ahead of time, and, as Grandfather tells the story, in past time.

And then time stands still, as this sixth section of *Famous Old People* ends:

> And now Grandfather perceived that little Alice had fallen fast asleep, with her head upon his footstool. Indeed, as Clara observed, she had been sleeping from the time of Sir Hovenden Walker's expedition against Quebec, until the death of Governor Burnet—a period of about eigh-teen years. And yet, after so long a nap, sweet little Alice was still a golden-haired child, of scarcely five years old. "It puts me in mind," said Laurence, "of the story of the enchanted princess, who slept many hundred years, and awoke as young and beautiful as ever." (106–7)

Just as Laurence's enchanted princess can bypass the boundaries of time without aging or losing her hold on common epistemology, so Cotton Mather can cross several boundaries of time at once, and so little Alice can nap for eighteen years yet remain five years old. Again, one of Grandfather's sketches privileges the limitless nature of reality.

The seventh section begins with a discussion of "fashions and manners . . . introduced from England into the provinces" (108) and their relation to boundaries of time. In his descriptions of festivals, balls, and clothing, Grandfather points to "a general change in social life" (108). Grandfather's chair is not spared a make-over in accordance with the tastes of the times, and, once it is adorned, "'Most people mistook it for a chair of the latest London fashion'" (111). Grandfather uses this perception of the chair as "'an example, that there is almost always an old and time-worn substance, under all the glittering show of new invention'" (111). Where "fashions and manners" may change superficially, the "old and time-worn substance" always remains. Underneath all the "grotesque caparison" of fashion stands "Charley's sturdy little figure" (110). In this passage, Grandfather stresses the durability and tenacity of the past, illustrating that the boundaries of time serve only "fashions and manners." They cannot stop the flow of time or isolate the present time as the exclusive reality.

Grandfather moves from fashion to war with "The Provincial Muster," in which New England uses alchemy to prepare a war expedition against Louisbourg, "a fortified city, on the Island of Cape Breton, near Nova Scotia" (113). To fund the troops, "'the legislature immediately sent out a huge quantity of paper money, with which, as if by magic spell, the governor hoped to get possession of all the old cannon, powder and balls, rusty swords and muskets, and every thing else that would be serviceable in killing Frenchmen'" (114).

Magic is needed to begin the war effort, as are the weapons of the past: "'Nothing now was so valuable as arms, of whatever style and fashion they might be. The bellows blew, and the hammer clanged continually upon the anvil, while the blacksmiths were repairing the broken weapons of other wars'" (115). These weapons enable New Englanders to cross into the past using the weapons of their ancestors, "'the early Puritans,'" "'Miles Standish's soldiers,'" the fighters long dead whose swords were now " 'corroded with rust, and stained with the blood of King Philip's war' " (115). In this way, " 'tall, lanky, awkward fellows' " (115), men with " 'rough faces and sturdy frames' " that would have made " 'a trained officer of Europe' " laugh " 'till his sides had ached' " (116), are changed into skilled, victorious soldiers.

With money fueled by magic and arms from the past, the war effort is so successful that its general, " 'a wealthy merchant, named William Pepperell' " (115), is transformed into Sir William Pepperell because of his victory. An aggression by untrained civilians against a fortified city with walls " 'of immense height and strength . . . defended by hundreds of heavy cannon' " (113) can succeed; money can turn into weaponry; "awkward fellows" can metamorphose into worthy fighters; and a merchant can become a baronet. Such transformations spring from a "flagrant abstraction from time" (Colacurcio 520).

In "The Provincial Muster," Grandfather's narrative begins to reveal the powerful effect perceptions of time have on historical events and on our perception of these events. The examples of Ezekiel Cheever, the procession of the Boston boys, Cotton Mather, and the changing forms of fashion and manners prime readers to see beyond time's boundaries and to begin to perceive that such boundaries may be arbitrarily imposed. The weapons of the past not only fire the efforts of the soldiers, but they also link past, present, and future wars, weapons, and peoples. Grandfather's privileging of temporality has been constant in *Famous Old People*. In "The Provincial Muster" the stakes are higher than ever before, as our views of history, life, and death—not schooling, not the smallpox inoculation, not fashions and manners— are significantly altered by Grandfather's shaping of our perceptions of time.

This escalation of perception continues in the ninth section of *Famous Old People*, as Grandfather sits in his chair on Thanksgiving eve:

> He felt that this was to be set down as one of the good Thanksgivings of his life. In truth, all his former Thanksgivings had borne their part in the present one; for, his years of infancy, and youth, and manhood, with their blessings and their griefs, had flitted before him, while he sat silently in the great chair. Vanished scenes had been pictured in the air.

The forms of departed friends had visited him. Voices, to be heard no more on earth, had sent an echo from the infinite and the eternal. These shadows, if such they were, seemed almost as real to him, as what was actually present—as the merry shouts and laughter of the children—as their figures, dancing like sunshine before his eyes.

He felt that the past was not taken from him. The happiness of former days was a possession forever. And there was something in the mingled sorrow of his lifetime, that became akin to happiness, after being long treasured in the depths of his heart. There it underwent a change, and grew more precious than pure gold. (121)

In this passage, we are told what we have been shown in earlier sketches: not only is the past an essential part of the present, but it is as "real . . . as what was actually present." In addition, memory has the properties of alchemy because it can transform "mingled sorrow" into happiness. Time is so powerful that it transforms people (from infancy to old age), transforms emotion, and easily transcends the boundaries that humankind has devised to contain it. Grandfather's musings here are not accessible to his grandchildren and so are private, personal, and specific. We move from temporality and American history to temporality and personal history. This move from many lives to one life continues the privileging of temporality and ensures our understanding that "former days" are "a possession forever," whether those days be in our lives or in the remote past.

"The Acadian Exiles," the final sketch of *Famous Old People*, attracts Grandfather's special attention because, "among all the events of the Old French War, Grandfather thought that there was none more interesting" than the Acadians being cast out into the world (124): "All their dwellings and churches were burnt, their cattle were killed, and the whole country was laid waste, so that none of them might find shelter or food in their old homes, after the departure of the English. One thousand of the prisoners were sent to Massachusetts" (124–25).

The Acadians lose their homes forever, lose family and friends, and are banished to another country with a foreign language. Upon their arrival in Massachusetts, they are completely out of their time: "'Every tie between these poor exiles and the world seemed to be cut off at once'" (126). "'Left to themselves, on a foreign strand'" (125),

their plight is rife with "'cruelty [and] . . . outrage'" (128), qualities that Grandfather stresses so heavily that "little Alice . . . burst
forth a-sobbing," and we are told that "Grandfather had touched her
sympathies more than he intended" (128).

By the end of the sketch, Grandfather's story has "made the children
feel the blessing of a secure and peaceful hearth" (129), a moral markedly disproportionate to Grandfather's graphic description. Surely "the
blessing of a secure and peaceful hearth" can be realized without a
tale of cruelty and outrage that terrorizes a five-year-old. If Grandfather's purpose in relating this event ("among all the events of the
Old French War, Grandfather thought that there was none more interesting" [124]) is proportionate to his tale, then the purpose must be
one he sees as essential for the children's education, one well worth a
temporary emotional upset.

Immediately before "The Acadian Exiles," we learned from Grandfather's musings that "former days" are "a possession forever" (121),
and so the Acadians' story becomes a possession of the children's that
vividly depicts the possibility of people blasted out of their world and
time. Since the past is as "real . . . as what was actually present" (121),
the children, as they hear "The Acadian Exiles," must add its cruelty
and outrage into their immediate reality and their pool of possibilities
offered by time. Grandfather's previous sketches have built up to the
terrible truth of "The Acadian Exiles." His steady emphasis on temporality, combined with his retelling of history, insists on "the full reality
of all times and places" (Colacurcio 520).

Nina Baym sees Grandfather's "purpose in attempting to reconstruct
history" (Shape 89) as providing "a way of understanding the present
by interpreting it in terms of past causes," helping "them to realize
that their own lives are not passed in a timeless present, but transpire in a temporal framework that extends beyond the limits of their
own transient existences. The learning of history is of a piece with the
inevitable transition from childhood to maturity, when discrete moments become related to past and future, and unthinking experience
is overlaid by reflection. History, in this view, is knowledge that we
cannot help but acquire, but much depends on the method by which
it is acquired" (Shape 89–90). For Baym, Grandfather's purpose "is
helping the children accept their mortality" (Shape 90), (surely worth

some sobbing on Alice's part). If the children also learn that their lives "transpire in a temporal framework that extends beyond the limits of their own transient existences," then Grandfather teaches them not only acceptance of their mortality but also realization of their *immortality*, as long as they bear in mind the fluid boundaries of time and reality.

Lest the children neglect this essential condition of their education, the chair finally passes to Thomas Hutchinson, who "'desired . . . to restore the chair, as much as possible, to its original aspect, such as it had appeared, when it was first made out of the Earl of Lincoln's oak-tree'" (137). Hutchinson's desire to restore the chair (and thus make it timeless) is the result of his knowing "'all the adventures and vicissitudes through which the old chair had passed'" (137). This knowledge is "high praise indeed," because "to know about 'the old chair' is, in the symbolism of the whole work, to know about the moving center of historical significance in early Massachusetts" (Colacurcio 419).

Despite this knowledge and the inspirational presence of the chair, Hutchinson's history of Massachusetts is unaided by "'any such extraordinary inspiration'" (137), for, says Grandfather, "'a duller piece of composition never came from any man's pen'" (138) and his "'visions of hereditary rank, for himself and other aristocratic colonists,'" have existence nowhere "'but among the red embers of the fire, before which he was sitting'" (139).

How is it that Hutchinson can be "in touch with the deepest realities of New England experience and assumptions" (Colacurcio 420) and yet fail to see where these realities will lead? "Only by a radical failure of historical imagination," according to Colacurcio, a failure to "grasp the real nature and force" of the New Englanders (420), one that will be more damningly portrayed in *Liberty Tree*. By neglecting his knowledge of the past, Hutchinson denies himself any realization of the future. He is left a dying old man with his foolish and limited dreams "'crumbled . . . to ashes'" (139). As long as the children do not underestimate the reality of all times, do not let their historical imaginations fail, their understanding, unlike Hutchinson's, will extend "beyond the limits of their own transient existences" (Baym, *Shape* 90).

After Hutchinson's dreams have crumbled, Grandfather looks "at his watch, which hung within a beautiful little ebony Temple, supported by four Ionic columns," and then sends the children to bed, telling them that " 'Grandfather has put you to sleep, already, by his stories about these Famous Old People!' " (139), thus ending the book. The description of Grandfather's watch, the final image of *Famous Old People*, is a striking one that enshrines time in a Greek temple. Proportion in design revealed the cosmic order to the Greek eye; therefore, the watch reminds the children of a people who recognized and valued the cosmic order.

Yet the watch also marks the reality of the present time, while Grandfather's glance at his watch implies he has lost track of time while storytelling. Hawthorne's highly self-conscious interest in time allows him to teach his audience history and mortality; the flagrant abstractions from time and the concept of limitless realities also permit Hawthorne's entrance into the combination of the actual and the imaginary, the neutral territory where he gained authority, confidence, and strength of artistic discourse. It is fitting Hawthornean irony that *Famous Old People* ends with a quick glance at a fictional watch accurately marking off time in the timeless world of Grandfather's chair.

Liberty Tree

"Has the youthful reader grown weary of Grandfather's stories about his Chair?" begins the preface to *Liberty Tree* (143), the only preface in the three works that is addressed directly to the reader. It is smooth, imaginative, and effective, combining a brief outline of the coming events of *Liberty Tree* with an affectionate description of Grandfather's chair: "Amid all these wonderful matters, we shall not lose sight of Grandfather's Chair. On its sturdy oaken legs, it trudges diligently from one scene to another, and seems always to thrust itself in the way, with most benign complacency, whenever a historical personage happens to be looking round for a seat. The excellent old Chair! Let the reader make much of it, while he may; for with this little volume Grandfather concludes its history, and withdraws it from the public eye" (144).

With "the excellent old Chair!" and the admonitory "let the reader make much of it, while he may," the language borders on the nostalgic. Both the chair and the author have trudged diligently through two volumes of stories. This may account for the relaxed language of the preface, language that portrays the chair at its most personified and thus its most powerful.

In the first section of the book, Grandfather paces the carpet, a storm rages outside, and, "with every puff of the wind," the fire leaps "laughing and rejoicing at the shrieks of the wintry storm" (145). The New Year's setting, Grandfather's unrest, nature's unrest, and the spirit of the fire rejoicing in the tumult—all indicate change. Calvin Earl Schorer correctly sees "the stormy New Year's weather" as a sign of "the approaching revolutionary days" (83). Even Grandfather's chair is changing, its shadow beginning to "quiver, and leap, and dance" (145), causing little Alice to try "to catch hold of the flickering shadow; for to children of five years old, a shadow seems almost as real as a substance" (145). Alice's inability to distinguish between substance and shadow makes Grandfather's stories particularly effective for her: by reaching back into the past, he arrives at a mixed reality that is part substance and part shadowy, remote times.

Charley is also more receptive to Grandfather's stories than he has been. " 'It would be better to hear stories about the chair,' " he says, confined indoors by the storm, " 'than to sit doing nothing, and thinking of nothing' " (146). Charley is out of sorts (and thus even more prepared for a story), because he cannot use his New Year's gift from Grandfather, "a splendid sled . . . honored with the title of Grandfather's Chair, which was painted in golden letters on each of the sides" (146). The well-named sled is a vehicle like Grandfather's chair, able to pass rapidly from one place to another, to move through time quickly. Charley is eager to put the sled to its literal and metaphorical uses. Since the weather prevents the former (and so he must "sit doing nothing"), he will settle for the latter (and at least not sit "thinking of nothing").

Alice and Charley are unaware of the effect that the *Grandfather's Chair* and *Famous Old People* stories have had on them, though the reader sees the children's heightened receptivity to new stories.

Laurence, the oldest and sharpest of the children, is much more conscious of what he has learned. His request for more stories reveals that knowledge: " 'The old chair has begun another year of its existence, today,' said Laurence. 'We must make haste, or it will have a new history to be told before we finish the old one' " (147). The oxymoron "new history" suggests that the reader, like Laurence, now understands that the boundaries of time are fluid: what is considered history could have occurred three hours or three centuries ago. Grandfather has trained his auditors well. Laurence already understands that history is dependent on how one looks at it and from whom one learns it.

Before Grandfather begins his story, Alice is convinced that "the lion's head was nodding at her, and that it looked as if it were going to open its wide jaws, and tell a story" (147). The lion's head does not speak at this moment, "and as there was no record or tradition of its having spoken, during the whole existence of the chair," Grandfather does not "consider it worth while to wait" for it to do so (147). This scene foreshadows the end of *Liberty Tree*, where the lion's head does indeed speak to Grandfather. The scene also stresses that the absence of records and traditions—Grandfather's tools—does not rule out the chair's history of speaking. Grandfather leans too heavily on the information he has and so will be caught unawares or, at the very least, will seem to be caught unawares, when the lion's head does speak to him.

For the moment, however, Grandfather relates the circumstances surrounding the Stamp Act and New England's reactions:

> "The former history of our chair, my children, has given you some idea of what a harsh, unyielding, stern set of men the old Puritans were. For a good many years back, however, it had seemed as if these characteristics were disappearing. But no sooner did England offer wrong to the colonies, than the descendants of the early settlers proved that they had the same kind of temper as their forefathers. The moment before, New England appeared like a humble and loyal subject of the crown; the next instant, she showed the grim, dark features of an old king-resisting Puritan." (150–51)

Grandfather rightly says that "it had seemed" as if the characteristics were disappearing. He is aware that such characteristics never disappear completely, but are recycled with time. Had England learned from the lessons of the past, the Stamp Act never would have been attempted; England would have remembered and expected the transformation of New England from "humble and loyal subject of the crown" to "old king-resisting Puritan."

Resistance to the Stamp Act leads to meetings under " 'an old elm-tree . . . which stood near the corner of Essex street, opposite the Boylston market,' " and the hanging of figures in effigy on the tree (152). The effigies " 'in square-skirted coats and small-clothes . . . looked like real men' " (152). Grandfather describes the effigies as " 'strange fruit' " of the tree. Their very alterity helps to disguise the real fruit of the liberty tree, the fruit of time. By neglecting to learn from the past, England has neglected to learn that change occurs with time and so is unable to foresee the future. In ignoring the past, England has ignored time, and thus strange fruit is indeed born in New England.

More fruits of the tree appear in the third section of *Liberty Tree*, which introduces the first formal sketch of the book, "The Hutchinson Mob," and features Lieutenant Governor Hutchinson, whom Grandfather had effectively dismissed in *Famous Old People*. Here, Hutchinson's loyalty to the king conflicts with his New England interests. Laurence prepares us for Grandfather's contemptuous crushing of Hutchinson by remarking, " 'I should think . . . as Mr. Hutchinson had written the history of our Puritan forefathers, he would have known what the temper of the people was, and so have taken care not to wrong them' " (153). Laurence shows that he, at least, knows that one should learn from the past, that even a child can see that Hutchinson should have known what would happen. Grandfather replies that Hutchinson " 'trusted in the might of the king of England' " (153) and tells a story illustrating Hutchinson's lack of understanding.

Qualities of the mob that attack Hutchinson's home associate it with the fire spirit that was introduced, earlier in *Famous Old People*, as "a kindly, cheerful, sociable spirit, sympathizing with mankind, and knowing that to create warmth is but one of the good offices which are expected from it" (73) and that reappeared, at the beginning of *Liberty Tree*, leaping "upward from the hearth, laughing and rejoicing at the shrieks of the wintry storm" (145). The mob's weapon is fire, and their actions and emotions are similar to the wood fire's activity: "'The mob, meanwhile, were growing fiercer and fiercer, and seemed ready even to set the town on fire, for the sake of burning the king's friends out of house and home. And yet, angry as they were, they sometimes broke into a loud roar of laughter, as if mischief and destruction were their sport'" (155). Individual New Englanders make up the mob, but taken together they are as powerful and unpredictable as the fireside spirit. The target of their almost supernatural emotions is "'the lieutenant governor's splendid mansion, . . . a large brick house, decorated with Ionic pilasters'" (155). The Ionic pilasters recall the earlier description of Grandfather's watch at the end of *Famous Old People* and show Hutchinson living in a house that is in the past, just as Hutchinson himself, inside the house, is in the past and unaware of the present and future.

Because of his lack of awareness, Hutchinson's home is destroyed and his family forced to flee. As he looks out the window at the mob, Hutchinson feels "'that the wrath of the people was a thousand-fold more terrible than the wrath of a king'" (157). With Hutchinson frozen at the window, Grandfather passes the judgment intended to teach the children what Hutchinson neglected to learn: "'That was a moment when a loyalist and an aristocrat, like Hutchinson, might have learnt how powerless are kings, nobles, and great men, when the low and humble range themselves against them. King George could do nothing for his servant now. Had King George been there, he could have done nothing for himself. If Hutchinson had understood this lesson, and remembered it, he need not, in after years, have been an exile from his native country, nor finally have laid his bones in a distant land" (157). Hutchinson, having failed to use his valuable knowledge, has remained behind the times. We see him literally behind a window, looking at the future (the crowd) from the past (within his house), with past and future separated by no more than a clear pane of glass. The otherness of the wild mob can enter through that glass, the otherness of the future Hutchinson resisted.

Grandfather's reaction is strongest in this passage. To ignore the lessons of the past is bad enough, but to do so when one is "'more

familiar with the history of New England than any other man alive'"
(*Famous Old People* 137) makes Hutchinson contemptible. He is literally banished from the history of New England by dying and being
buried elsewhere.

It is fitting that Hutchinson, having completely failed to learn from
Grandfather's chair, loses it immediately after the mob scene. It next
appears under the Liberty Tree on a stormy day when Andrew Oliver
is forced to vow his disassociation from distributing the stamps. The
weather again matches events, though the setting is more dismal than
dangerous as Mr. Oliver appears "'haggard, disconsolate, and humbled
to the earth'" (160). Grandfather sympathizes with "'poor Mr. Oliver'"
(160), in marked contrast to his reaction to Hutchinson's distress:
"'But it was a sad day for poor Mr. Oliver,' observed Grandfather. 'From
his youth upward, it had probably been the great principle of his life,
to be faithful and obedient to the king. And now, in his old age, it must
have puzzled and distracted him, to find the sovereign people setting
up a claim to his faith and obedience'" (160). Mr. Oliver lacked the
information and benefit of study that Hutchinson had. Grandfather
can thus spare him sympathy as he finds himself out of time in his old
age. Unlike Hutchinson, he did not know about the chair.

After the Stamp Act's repeal in 1776, the chair moves to the British
Coffee House, "'in the midst of business and bustle'" (161), where
it "'was now continually occupied by some of the high tories, as the
king's friends were called'" (163). In the British Coffee House the
chair can continue to monitor the change in the times, since it is
"the moving center of historical significance in early Massachusetts"
(Colacurcio 419). The chair remains out of the action of *Liberty Tree*
for almost twenty pages. Its occupation of the British gathering place
parallels the British military's occupation of Boston, the background
of which Grandfather relates as he leads up to the next formal sketch,
"The Boston Massacre."

The sketch begins after "'two or three slight commotions'" (166)
and a false fire alarm have caused the gathering of a crowd that has "'a
presentiment that some strange event was on the eve of taking place'"
(167). When the times are about to change significantly, even from

one moment to the next, the sense of change becomes palpable. As British soldiers and New Englanders begin to clash, the narrative is stopped on the very threshold of change:

> "Oh, what a crisis had now arrived! Up to this very moment, the angry feelings between England and America might have been pacified. England had but to stretch out the hand of reconciliation, and acknowledge that she had hitherto mistaken her rights, but would do so no more. Then, the ancient bonds of brotherhood would again have been knit together, as firmly as in old times. The habit of loyalty, which had grown as strong as instinct, was not utterly overcome. The perils shared, and victories won, in the Old French War, when the soldiers of the colonies fought side by side with their comrades from beyond the sea, were unforgotten yet. England was still that beloved country which the colonists called their home. King George, though he had frowned upon America, was still reverenced as a father.
>
> But, should the king's soldiers shed one drop of American blood, then it was a quarrel to the death." (169)

The use of the phrase "up to this very moment" points to the Boston Massacre as the turning point in British and American relations and stresses the significance of time. Radical change can occur in a moment once its time has come. Americans will yield to their memories ("perils shared, and victories won . . . were unforgotten yet") and learn from the past if the British will do the same. Had the British learned from the Puritans' reactions, the time for a break between the countries would never have arrived. As the sketch ends, the blood shed by the British " 'was never forgotten nor forgiven by the people' " (170), and its effect crosses the boundaries of temporality. The bloodshed of the Boston Massacre is both the signal for "a quarrel to the death" (169) in 1770 and an event of history, a lesson of the past, the moment it occurs.

For the first time since the Acadians were banished by Grandfather, Alice is in "bewilderment and horror," because, "in his earnestness, he [Grandfather] had neglected to soften down the narrative, so that it might not terrify the heart of this unworldly infant" (170). Grandfather reproaches himself: " 'Oh, what a pity! Her heavenly nature has now received its first impression of earthly sin and violence! Well,

Clara, take her to bed, and comfort her'" (170). Despite Alice's "violent sobs" (170), Grandfather's reaction shows that Alice's loss of innocence is inevitable. It is, after all, only by knowing of earthly sin and violence that she will be able to accept her mortality and begin to understand herself and humankind.

The next evening, with Alice, presumably recovered, in attendance, Laurence begins the sixth section of Liberty Tree as he studies a book of portraits, a "New Year's gift from Grandfather," and examines "the portrait of a stern, grim-looking man, in plain attire, of much more modern fashion than that of the old Puritans," and whose face "might well have befitted one of those iron-hearted men" (173). Samuel Adams, the portrait's subject, is described by Grandfather as one in whom it "'seemed as if one of the ancient Puritans had been sent back to earth, to animate the people's hearts with the same abhorrence of tyranny, that had distinguished the earliest settlers'" (173). Adams, another of Hawthorne's male alchemists, has crossed the boundaries of time in both his physical and his rhetorical re-creation of the old Puritans. And, like William Phips of "The Sunken Treasure," Adams has gone from rags to riches. He begins as "'a poor man'" who "'earned his bread by a humble occupation'" (173) and becomes one whose "'tongue and pen . . . made the king of England tremble on his throne'" (174).

Adams is not alone in his transformation. "Many a New Englander, who had passed his boyhood and youth in obscurity," Grandfather remarks, "afterward attained to a fortune, which he never could have foreseen, even in his most ambitious dreams" (175–76):

> John Adams, the second president of the United States, and the equal of crowned kings, was once a school-master and country lawyer. Hancock, the first signer of the Declaration of Independence, served his apprenticeship with a merchant. Samuel Adams, afterwards governor of Massachusetts, was a small tradesman and a tax-gatherer. General Warren was a physician, General Lincoln, a farmer, and General Knox, a bookbinder. General Nathaniel Greene, the best soldier, except Washington, in the revolutionary army, was a Quaker and a black-smith. All these became illustrious men, and can never be forgotten in American history. (176)

The men to be admired by the children, the men who "can never be forgotten in American history," have undergone a permanent transformation, have been redefined and reconfigured.

People transform even more quickly, albeit temporarily, in the next formal sketch, "The Boston Tea Party," where "'a set of wild-looking figures'" are really conventional citizens (180). Their actions against British tea ships prefigure "the most gloomy time that Massachusetts had ever seen" (181). The immediate result of their transformations from civilian to savage is the transformation of Boston from port city to city under siege.

As war approaches, the transmutations multiply. Scores of Americans turn into minutemen "'ready to fight at a minute's warning'" (182), to metamorphose from civilians to soldiers at once. The battle of Lexington is a "'fatal volley, which . . . began the War of the Revolution'" (183). The volley, which takes place in a matter of minutes, wrenches the country from peace to war. As with the Boston Massacre, the actions of a moment change everything, becoming what Laurence would call "new history" as soon as they occur.

This series of transformations culminates in the introduction of General Washington, who evolves from a man in his time to an American legend who transcends time. Grandfather admires Washington more than any other man in the three children's histories. Washington is a conventional hero of American revolutionary history, but Grandfather's portrayal of him is less conventional. Washington's accomplishments here include the way he "'transformed this rough mob of country-people into the semblance of a regular army'" and the manner in which "'all business, with which he had any concern, seemed to regulate itself, as if by magic'" (187, 188). Grandfather thus locates Washington's power in his timelessness and ability to reconfigure reality.

Just before Washington's arrival at his Cambridge headquarters, Grandfather's chair mysteriously disappears from the British Coffee House (a sign that historical significance no longer rests with the British) and reappears at Washington's headquarters moments before the great man arrives. With the chair in his possession, Washington's movement from man to legend, the greatest transformation of *The Whole History*, can proceed. Supported by the transformations of Americans in the past and surrounded by Adams, Hancock, Warren, Knox, and Greene, who are undergoing transformations in the present, Washington can defeat the British, change the course of American history, and bring the reader to the denouement of both *Liberty Tree* and *The Whole History of Grandfather's Chair*. Such a change cannot help but interest Grandfather, who "thought that Boston had never witnessed a more interesting period than this, when the royal power was in its death agony, [and so] he determined to take a peep into the town, and imagine the feelings of those who were quitting it forever" (190). The last period of history that so caught Grandfather's interest was the Acadian exile. The significance of "The Acadian Exiles" is thus recalled for the last historical sketch of *Liberty Tree*.

In "The Tory's Farewell," Peter Oliver, "chief justice of Massachusetts under the crown" (191), having failed to understand the present, takes "'a parting look at objects that had been familiar to him from his youth'" (191) before he leaves America forever. Like his brother Andrew Oliver, who had been forced to swear an oath under the Liberty Tree, Peter Oliver is bewildered by the times: "'Can it be possible, that a few fleeting years have wrought such a change!'" (192). The changes, of course, have been brewing and calling attention to their presence for much longer, but Oliver has been unable to read the signs. As he bids Boston good-bye, "'deep love and fierce resentment burned in one flame within his breast'" (196). By not understanding his times, Peter Oliver has become a man lost in a permanently liminal state between two countries, neither one of which he can call his home. His world—New England under the Crown—no longer exists, and the country he is to go to, England, cannot replace what he has lost.

As if to underscore that England will be no surrogate home for Oliver and his fellows, Oliver is snubbed by Sir William Howe as he leaves Boston and thus has "a foretaste of the mortifications which the exiled New Englanders afterwards suffered from the haughty Britons. They were despised even by that country which they had served more faithfully than their own" (194). Oliver is carefully identified as an exiled New Englander (as opposed to Sir William Howe, a Briton) to make clear where he belongs and where he will not be permitted to stay.

Grandfather tells the children that Oliver was one of a thousand exiles and asks, " 'Were they not the most unfortunate of men?' " (196). Like the Acadian exiles, Oliver and his kind are victims of powerful forces of time and change, but, unlike that of the Acadian exiles, their story rouses no sympathy from the children. (Indeed, little Alice, usually a reliable source of sympathy, can think to ask only if General Washington had brought the chair back from Boston.) Because the exiled New Englanders were loyal to another country, no matter how sincere their choice was, they deliberately risked banishment from the shores of New England, unlike the Acadians, who had no choice at all and remained loyal to their land. Oliver is portrayed, not as a villain, but as a misguided, unfortunate casualty of the American Revolution. The children cannot pity him, because the very events that cast Oliver into the loveless universe result in the defeat of the British and the triumph of American heroes.

With the major events of American history now in the past, the chair is semiretired to a barbershop together with " 'a stuffed alligator, a rattlesnake's skin, a bundle of Indian arrows, an old-fashioned matchlock gun, a walking-stick of Governor Winthrop's, a wig of old Cotton Mather's, and a colored print of the Boston Massacre' " (198). Amid this eccentric collection of historical relics the chair remains for the next eighteen years. Grandfather gives the children a rapid, miscellaneous telling of events that followed the British evacuation and eventually resulted in Samuel Adams's election as governor in 1794. After his election, Adams noticed the chair and " 'made minute researches into its history, and ascertained what a succession of excellent and famous people had occupied it' " (203). (To be "well acquainted" with the chair is Grandfather's highest compliment [203].) The chair remains with Adams until his death, when it passes to Grandfather himself.

Now that the chair's adventures are ended, Laurence, who has "learned all its history, . . . was not satisfied": " 'Oh, how I wish that the chair could speak!' cried he. 'After its long intercourse with mankind—after looking upon the world for ages—what lessons of golden wisdom it might utter! It might teach a private person how to lead a good and happy life—or a statesman how to make his country prosperous!'" (204). Schooled by Grandfather, Laurence demands more than a history lesson from the chair. "Its long intercourse with mankind" must result in a rule or two that teaches one how to operate in the world.

Laurence's wish gives way to the final sketch of *Liberty Tree* and the culminating sketch of *The Whole History of Grandfather's Chair*. Grandfather determines "to have recourse to fable," and, "warning the children that they must not mistake this story for a true one," he relates "what we shall call—'Grandfather's Dream'" (205). The use of the words "fable," "story," "true" story, and "dream" blur the distinctions of veracity in storytelling, which had already been called into question by Grandfather's mixing of fact and imagination and his emphasis on the full reality of all times and places. If we read Grandfather's warning literally, a fable can be a dream and a story, but it cannot be a true story. Why, though, should we accept these boundaries? Other boundaries have been transcended in *The Whole History of Grandfather's Chair*. As for the truth of the sketch that ends the collection, hints have been dropped throughout the text about the chair's speaking in addition to its ability to hear, move, and judge the importance of various places and people. Thus, before the chair speaks, the reader has been prepared for this possibility. Grandfather's warning that the children "must not mistake this story for a true one" (205) rests less on the elocutionary ability of the chair and more, perhaps, on the major difference between this sketch and all the others: the lack of any historical personages as characters and the presence of Grandfather himself. Perhaps because this sketch involves Grandfather as a character, it must be a dream, a fable, a story that is not "true" until someone else tells it.

The setting of "Grandfather's Dream" signals the presence of the unusual. The normally active wood fire has "'crumbled into heavy embers, among which the little flames danced, and quivered, and sported about, like fairies'" (205). In past sketches, the fire's behavior has been an indicator of coming events; here, the comparison of flames to fairies suggests magic. Grandfather, who usually gazes into the fire as he meditates, has "'closed his eyes, for the sake of meditating more profoundly'" (205). On the margins between sleeping and dreaming, Grandfather is outside the boundaries of time and so in the proper place to meet the chair.

Aided by "'rays of firelight'" (206), the chair comes to life and tells Grandfather the names of others with whom it has conversed, running down a partial list of characters who have appeared in *Grandfather's Chair*, *Famous Old People*, and *Liberty Tree*. The chair, as Laurence surmised, has benefited from its experiences and so on several occasions gave sound advice that reflected its historical imagination and understanding of the fluid boundaries of time and reality: "'Cotton Mather had several conversations with me, and derived great benefit from my historical reminiscences. In the days of the Stamp Act, I whispered in the ear of Hutchinson, bidding him to remember what stock his countrymen were descended of, and to think whether the spirit of their forefathers had utterly departed from them'" (207).

Good historian that he is, Grandfather inquires as to the lack of records and traditions regarding the chair's past conversations, and the chair points out its tendency to avoid "'the most suitable moments for unclosing my lips'" (207). Indeed, it tells Grandfather, that tendency is so strong that, "'though my words make a pretty strong impression at the moment, . . . my auditors invariably remember them only as a dream'" (208). Grandfather himself, the chair continues, will probably have the same impression the next morning.

Having spoken of the past and referred to the future, the chair, placing itself clearly in the concerns of the present, requests a new cushion, a coat of varnish, and an adjustment to one of its joints. After promising to attend to these matters, Grandfather, in what seems to be a deliberate rewording of Laurence's request, appeals to the chair for guidance: "'During an existence of more than two centuries, you have had a familiar intercourse with men who were esteemed the wisest of their day. Doubtless, with your capacious understanding, you have treasured up many an invaluable lesson of wisdom. You certainly have had time enough to guess the riddle of life. Tell us poor mortals, then, how we may be happy!'" (208–9). Grandfather's wording clearly recalls Laurence's request. Can it be that Grandfather, who has failed to predict the chair's speaking, has also found himself, with Laurence, demanding a justification of history? To accept this conjecture means placing Grandfather's historical understanding on the same level as Laurence's, a conclusion belied by Grandfather's years, wisdom, and role as educator.

In order to approach the demand for more than a history lesson from the experiences of the chair (and thus from the learning of history), Grandfather either poses Laurence's question to the chair or tells the children that he has done so. Grandfather, it would seem, already knows the answer to this question, but prefers to have the answer, terse and simple as it may be, come from the chair itself: " 'As long as I have stood in the midst of human affairs,' said the chair, with a very oracular enunciation, 'I have constantly observed that Justice, Truth, and Love, are the chief ingredients of every happy life' " (209). This "pre-critical truism" (Colacurcio 521) appears to surprise Grandfather, who protests, " 'This is no secret. Every human being is born with the instinctive knowledge of it' " (209). Grandfather's response equally surprises the chair, which, from " 'the dealings of man with man, and nation with nation,' " has never guessed that " 'this all-important secret' " (209) was known and, having told what it knows, refuses to speak further and ends the sketch.

Pleased with the dream, the children demand " 'a new dream, every night' " (210). Grandfather, not unlike the chair, refuses and declares, "Here ended the history, real or fabulous, of Grandfather's Chair" (210). Like the chair, Grandfather has told all that he is going to tell at present. The children must wait for additional knowledge as they mature and "have ample time to learn that Life is not Conclusion" (Colacurcio 522). As a last reminder or perhaps a clue to future historical stories, Grandfather leaves the children with "real or fabulous," as though one may be easily mistaken for the other. And, in the text of *The Whole History of Grandfather's Chair* at least, the distinction is not a clear one, nor is it meant to be so.

The privileging of alternative realities in the collection insists on an artistic territory where the boundaries of time have lost their rigidity. To reach this place himself and change from Nathaniel Hawthorne, thirty-six-year-old, financially struggling, unsuccessful author, into Nathaniel Hawthorne, teller of stories, Hawthorne allowed himself to be displaced as narrator. He substituted Grandfather—an older, wiser, and more traditional figure, a man respected in his culture. If Grandfather was Hawthorne, then Hawthorne could not solely be that employee of the Custom House, that disappointment to his ancestors, that frustrated and struggling bachelor, that writer unable to earn a living through his art.

Grandfather's authority in the stories creates a model in which the narrator rules, since the narrative is his domain of power. With this power, Hawthorne completed his transformation, escaped the limits of temporality, and, armed with imaginative authority, located what he would later define as "a neutral territory, somewhere between the real world and fairy-land, where the Actual and the Imaginary may meet, and each imbue itself with the nature of the other" (*Scarlet Letter* 36). He would not confidently and publicly point to this territory until he wrote "The Custom House," the introduction to *The Scarlet Letter*, a full decade after *Grandfather's Chair*, *Famous Old People*, and *Liberty Tree* had been completed and published. In writing these children's books, Hawthorne first located and acquainted himself with a reality where the real and the fabulous are conflated, a reality that lent itself to "a lively and entertaining narrative for children" (*Grandfather's Chair* 6). In his diligent and sincere attempt to write such narratives, Hawthorne managed to slip the bonds of the present and enter the full reality of all times and places.

CHAPTER TWO

The Denial of Invention:
Biographical Stories for Children

Biographical Stories for Children was first published in 1842 and "reissued, significantly revised, in 1851" (Pearce 296), along with *The Whole History of Grandfather's Chair*, as *True Stories from History and Biography*. *Biographical Stories* features an authoritative adult, Mr. Temple, telling stories about the childhood of famous people to his son, Edward, whose eye disorder keeps him confined, eyes covered, in a darkened room. The audience includes the boy's mother, Mrs. Temple, his adopted sister, Emily, and his older brother, George. Mr. Temple tells stories of Benjamin West, Sir Isaac Newton, Samuel Johnson, Oliver Cromwell, Benjamin Franklin, and Queen Christina of Sweden, all meant to enliven Edward's confinement and to educate and entertain the family audience and the book's intended youthful readers.

Unlike *The Whole History*, however, *Biographical Stories* has nothing as distinctive as the chair or as structured as the history of a country to help unite Mr. Temple's stories. The stories in the collection are sketchy and fragmented, and, in general, they reflect a lack of care in execution. The story frames are brief compared to those in *The Whole History* and, when expanded beyond a few lines, are censuring and moralistic. All in all, *Biographical Stories* is, not only of inferior quality when compared with *The Whole History*, but, with its ineffective frame and imperfectly rendered stories, an inferior work on its own.

Though Hawthorne began *Biographical Stories* at Brook Farm, "he tried in vain" to complete it there "but found the 'ferment' around him too disturbing" and so was unable to complete the work until a few months after he left the community (Schorer 11–12). Perhaps because of Brook Farm's atmosphere, perhaps because of his inability to finish the collection without interruption, Hawthorne did not turn the formula of frame and sketch in *Biographical Stories* into the polished interplay seen in *The Whole History*. He would not return to children's books until after the publication of *The Scarlet Letter*, when, as a mature and celebrated author, he would write *A Wonder Book for Boys and Girls*.

The Whole History and *Biographical Stories* differ greatly, despite Hawthorne's attempts to impose the same narrative formula on them. Unlike that of *The Whole History*, the structure of *Biographical Stories* forces Hawthorne to tell stories that concern famous people as children. Illness, magic, piety, obedience, transformations, and the relation of parent and child (indeed, with the exception of the Queen Christina story, the relation of father and son) are basic elements of childhood here. Childhood must be stressed because Hawthorne has lost the elasticity of subject that he retained in *The Whole History*. He has committed himself to stories of childhood, where organizational powers, and hence complex organization, are less important.

Limited as this structure is, chances for artistic success are further complicated by Hawthorne's treatment of Edward Temple's illness—an illness not severe enough to kill and thus consecrate him. Like Hawthorne, Edward Temple is confined in misery-inducing circumstances. Because of his blindfolded enclosure in a darkened room, Edward Temple's life is a kind of death but must be treated as a life. This treatment resists the sentimental, because Edward Temple is not dead and is not going to die from his illness. The very structure of the collection insists that Edward will not die, recover, or sicken further. All that remains to be portrayed are Edward's attempts at living his resignation, at hugging alienation close. Hawthorne thus populates the space in Edward's life and in his own with narration. That narration is unsuccessful because its purpose—to make resignation palatable—is such a bleak one. Throughout the collection, illness of children is a recurring and uneasy theme laced with a heavy morality designed to make the less fortunate accept their lot in life.

Hawthorne's inability to cure Edward Temple and himself (or perhaps his reluctance to cure Edward Temple because he could not cure himself), combined with his restlessness as he shuttled from the Custom House to Brook Farm and from eternal bachelorhood to the hope of marriage, prohibit any departure in the text. Reality takes a stranglehold in *Biographical Stories*, and Hawthorne rarely escapes into any alternative reality in its pages. With his life in disarray, his cultural position weak, and his writing still distant from the artistic and commercial success for which he yearned, Hawthorne employs certain fictive obstacles in *Biographical Stories* that prevent his entrance into the mediated world of the actual and the imaginary, the neutral territory most providential for his discourse.

The preface to the collection begins with the rationale for the stories: "If children are to be introduced to the eminent personages of times gone by, the most effectual method is, to begin the acquaintance with the childhood of those great men and women" (213). Such a sweetened form of learning causes a child to develop affection for the other child, and so "when, hereafter, the reader shall learn the deeds of their manhood, it will be with a portion of the interest which we feel in the lives of our early companions" (213). This more intimate approach makes history "real" and human rather than awesome and remote. Hawthorne's idea of sustained interest, relying as it does on time, history, memory, the familiar, and the role all play in one's education, recalls *The Whole History*, but it will not achieve the prominence here that it has in that work.

As he does in earlier prefaces, Hawthorne asserts his integrity and regard for the truth, concluding that he "hopes, therefore, that this little book may conscientiously be put into a child's hands, as a trustworthy authority respecting the personages of whom it treats" (214). The use of the word "conscientiously" suggests the deluge of morality to come and Hawthorne's own sentimental treatment of children. Hawthorne expands upon this in the final paragraph of the preface, maintaining that he writes children's books with a "deep sense of responsibility" and that he "regards children as sacred, and would not, for the world, cast anything into the fountain of a young heart, that might embitter and pollute its waters" (214). Most contemporary histories for children, in Hawthorne's view, retold history badly in addition to giving poor instruction in moral matters.[1] Concern for historical representation runs throughout Hawthorne's fictions. The sentimental pieties reflected in his vow to avoid pollution of history's lessons will continue in the text of *Biographical Stories*, but here Hawthorne uses them to discuss the place in popular culture for a writer of children's stories: "And, even in point of the reputation to be aimed at, juvenile literature is as well worth cultivating as any other. The writer, if he succeed in pleasing his little readers, may hope to be remembered by them till their own old age—a far longer period of literary existence than is generally attained, by those who seek immortality from the judgments of full grown men" (214). Hawthorne's desire to succeed in cultural competition and his sociological awareness of the growing split between elite ("the judgments of full grown men") and mass culture are clear. Equally clear are the significant roles that time, history, and memory will play in such achievement. Children's literature serves as an appropriate neutral territory for Hawthorne, a genre where the competition seems less fierce and the rewards just as great.

As the collection begins, Edward's eyes are bandaged, and he is banished to a darkened room. His blindness means all must "vanish" (215) until some later, unspecified time when he can see again. His illness, a form of magic that causes people and places to disappear, frightens and depresses him. Mrs. Temple, his mother, resists his mourning for his eyesight and, in the first of the moralizing platitudes with which she will attempt to comfort him and resign him to his lot, tells him: "'Your eyesight was a precious gift of Heaven, it is true; but you would do wrong to be miserable for its loss, even if there were no hope of regaining it. There are other enjoyments, besides what come to us through our eyes'" (216). In addition to this semantic comfort, with its teasing mention of "other enjoyments" that exist for the sightless (a literary escape from realism, a philosophical escape from an empiricist privileging of sight, a forecasting of the comforts of touch), Mrs. Temple reminds Edward that he will have the frequent company of his brother, George, "a fine, hardy lad, of a bold and ardent temper" (216), much like Charley of *The Whole History*, and "little Emily Robinson, . . . the daughter of one of Mr. Temple's dearest friends" (217). The boys would not know "the blessing of a sister, had not this gentle stranger come to teach them what it was" (217). What Emily herself will be taught will be of concern as *Biographical Stories* proceeds. Last of all, we meet Mr. Temple, who, "though invisible to Edward, . . . was standing close beside him" (217). Mrs. Temple's comfort to Edward was vague, but there was no question about her physical presence. Mr. Temple, who promises to tell a series of stories, offers no verbal comfort and cannot be sensed by Edward even when he is "close beside him." Not only have people and places vanished for Edward, but his father, the author of the coming stories and the locus of author-ity, has become invisible and omnipresent. From first mention, the father's power is ominous and seemingly limitless.

Before he starts his first story, Mr. Temple advises Edward to " 'see things within your own mind' " (220), a reference to inner vision that appears throughout the story of Benjamin West, which Mr. Temple goes on to tell.[2] The story itself is an imagined vision; Benjamin West's vision occurs inside the story; and the story is both heard and held within the heads of the listeners. It is not, however, the only type of vision impressed upon Mr. Temple's audience, nor is it the type of vision most readily offered to his audience. Mr. Temple uses a series of miscellaneous references to outer sight: " 'the eyes of many people were fixed' " (220–21); " 'delighted himself with gazing' " (221); " 'how beautiful she looks!' " (221); " 'took vast delight in looking' " (222); and " 'better than to gaze' " (222).

Mr. Temple's phrases, along with young Benjamin West's ability to use his eyes to paint what he sees, emphasize that Edward must adjust to his illness and resign himself to alienation from a world of paintings and sight. This alienation may or may not include distance from the kind of inner sight, or imagination, that aided Benjamin West in using his eyes as he did. Whether or not Edward's physical sightlessness will also include spiritual sightlessness remains unclear as long as his blindness is diagnosed as temporary. In the meantime, Edward must try not to mourn his separation from the world of eyesight, a world that allows young Benjamin's drawing, a process so unknown to him that, after sketching his sister, he says he has been "'stealing the baby's face'" (222). The act of painting or drawing allows one to use magic, to steal another's face and thus another's identity. Without eyesight, then, one's identity is limited and isolated, unable to use sight to absorb elements of surrounding identities and experiences.

As an adolescent, young Benjamin develops an eye problem and, like Edward, is confined to a darkened room. His chamber, however, is not totally dark, nor are his eyes bandaged. His observations of light and dark while he is confined result in his development of "'a Camera Obscura, or Magic Lantern, . . . [which] was of great advantage to him in drawing landscapes'" (226). Not only is Benjamin creative while confined; but, unlike Edward's case, the "'slight attack of fever, which confined him to his bed'" (225), is soon over, and he is released from his enclosure. Once free, Benjamin seeks approval of his painting from his Quaker community. With this approval his art has received community authority. He leaves "'all the places and persons whom he had hitherto known,—and returned to them no more'" (227). His imagination has set him free in the world; his community has given him the authority to leave his past behind him; and Benjamin is allowed to develop "'into the most distinguished English painter of his day'" (228–29). His transformation is much admired by others ("'The story of his life is almost as wonderful as a fairy tale'" [228]), and the story concludes: "'Let us each make the best use of our natural abilities, as Benjamin West did; and with the blessing of Providence, we shall arrive at some good end. As for fame, it is but little matter whether we acquire it or not'" (229). Hawthorne's hopeful reference to literary fame in the collection's preface and West's achievement of fame undercut this assertion. Here and in the preface, fame suggests cultural acceptance and acknowledgment of one's art. Such conspicuous cultural success mattered. Though Hawthorne here brushes fame aside as "but little matter whether we acquire it or not," we know from his letters and journal entries that he could not easily do this in daily life. In the same way, counseling Edward toward inner vision is easier than his locating, developing, and valuing that vision as much as his eyesight.

The text relies on Edward's willingness to see the role inner vision played in West's life and accomplishments. He must move beyond the tale of a boy who suffers only brief eye problems and earns freedom and fame by using his inner and outer eye to see things and render them. Not unreasonably feeling sorry for himself after what can be read as a lesson in what he lacks, Edward says he feels " 'alone in a dark world' " (229) and turns to his community, his authority figures, for comfort. Mrs. Temple tells him, " 'You must have faith. . . . Faith is the soul's eyesight; and when we possess it, the world is never dark nor lonely' " (229). Edward's response to this reply is not given, nor do we hear any response by Mr. Temple to Edward's plea. Mr. Temple's belief that Edward's only recourse is resignation has been delivered in the tale, while Mrs. Temple's urge for inner vision is neither supported nor contradicted by the rest of the family.

In the next frame, which prefaces the story of Isaac Newton, Emily teaches Edward to knit. He spends an hour or two learning to create without outer vision, and he changes in the process. Afterward, he has a "very bright expression upon his lips," and he tells his family he can see them with his " 'mind's eye' " (231). We are meant to think that Edward has moved beyond the dark loneliness of the previous night, an interpretation supported by his ability to create despite the loss of his eyesight and by his assertion that, not only is he aware of an inner eye, but he can use it to see those he loves. Yet Edward's ability to express himself has become even more limited: his face shrinks to feature only a closed mouth as an indicator of his feelings. By knitting, Edward associates himself with the image of the writer/creator who knits together fact and imagination to form fiction and with the nineteenth-century woman who performed these steady, repetitious tasks in her own domestic confinement as a defense against her alienation/isolation, which felt like illness. The effect of the knitting metaphor is further complicated by Edward's never knitting again in *Biographical Stories*. Whether Edward has truly understood the nature of his inner vision or is defending himself against the approach of the darkness and loneliness he fears by occupying himself in whatever way is offered is decidedly ambiguous.[3]

The Isaac Newton story that follows is a fragmented collection of anecdotes from Newton's life. He invents a miniature mill; he spends his time "'gazing at the heavenly bodies through a telescope'" (236); he treats his dog kindly after the animal accidentally causes his notes to be burned; he is modest about his great store of knowledge. The tale ends with a prediction of Newton's immortality: "'He has left a fame behind him, which will be as endurable as if his name were written in letters of light, formed by the stars upon the midnight sky'" (237). Newton, like West, achieves fame and immortality because of his ability to think, his insight. The image of Newton's name written in the sky is an eye reference and a link to his telescope gazing. Edward seizes on these images and decides that Newton's life could never be his own: "'It must have been beautiful,' said Edward, 'to spend whole nights in a high tower, as Newton did, gazing at the stars, and the comets, and the meteors. But what would Newton have done, had he been blind? or if his eyes had been no better than mine?'" (237–38). With no help from Mr. Temple to show that Newton did not need great eyes to be a great thinker, Edward can only locate himself in Newton's isolation "in a high tower." Again he turns to his family for help, and again Mr. Temple says nothing, while Mrs. Temple replies, "'Why, even then, my dear child,' observed Mrs. Temple, 'he would have found out some way of enlightening his mind, and of elevating his soul. But, come! little Emily is waiting to bid you good night. You must go to sleep, and dream of seeing all our faces.' 'But how sad it will be, when I awake!' murmured Edward" (238). Mrs. Temple cannot help or heal Edward. Even her assurance that Newton, if blinded, "would have found out some way of enlightening his mind" fails to be at all specific. Her inability to nurture her child properly is implied by Edward's illness, while her inability to answer his questions after the stories are told reveals her lack of authority. She is not an author herself (Mr. Temple always tells the stories), and she is unable to tell her own story, much less fully answer questions concerning Mr. Temple's patriarchal narrations.

The next day George and Edward argue, and, as they sit sullenly in the room, "Mr. Temple, without seeming to notice any of these circumstances" (239), begins the story of the life of Samuel Johnson. Empowered by his position at the center of this phallocentric, logocentric world, Mr. Temple knows that something is amiss without being told. He rarely speaks outside the telling of the stories, and his strategies of narration are antidialogic: he is one person always narrating the world for others.

In contrast to this father's perfect authority, Samuel Johnson, son of Michael Johnson, is " 'almost blind,' " with a " 'seamed and distorted' " face (240), is afflicted by a " 'tremulous motion' " (241) of his head, and is dressed in shabby clothing. Like Edward, he is near blind, but, unlike Edward, he is " 'conscious of uncommon sense and ability, which, in his own opinion, entitled him to great respect from the world' " (240). Thus he is proud, ill, and of singular aspect. These qualities commingle when he refuses to work at his father's bookstall. His father, Michael Johnson, takes refuge in a curse when he hears his son's refusal: " 'Well, Sam,' said Mr. Johnson, as he took his hat and staff, 'if, for the sake of your foolish pride, you can suffer your poor sick father to stand all day in the noise and confusion of the market, when he ought to be in his bed, I have no more to say. But you will think of this, Sam, when I am dead and gone!' " (241).

The paternal curse works, and before the day is over Sam begs for forgiveness: " 'Oh, I have been a cruel son!' thought he, within his own heart. 'God forgive me! God forgive me!' " (243). Despite his plea, the boy is not yet ready for divine forgiveness:

> "But God could not yet forgive him; for he was not truly penitent. Had he been so, he would have hastened away, that very moment, to Uttoxeter, and have fallen at his father's feet, even in the midst of the crowded market-place. There he would have confessed his fault, and besought Mr. Johnson to go home, and leave the rest of the day's work to him. But such was Sam's pride and natural stubbornness, that he could not bring himself to this humiliation. Yet he ought to have done so, for his own sake, and for his father's sake, and for God's sake." (243)

That Sam's sake here is linked with God's and his father's reveals the degree to which his behavior should match the moral expectations of the two fathers.

The images of a humiliation-demanding God, a martyred father, and another father who would tell such a story supposedly to reconcile two quarreling children form a triumvirate of dominating moral agents. The demands of the father may appear reasonable (spending the day selling books), but their complexity emerges when these demands are denied, and are denied by a hitherto obedient but proud and deformed boy shy of the prolonged public gaze. Punishment immediately begins, and the punishment for disobedience not only is greater than any temporary humiliation but is also ultimately administered by the son himself:

> "From his boyhood upward, until the latest day of his life, he never forgot the story of Uttoxeter market. Often, when he was a scholar of the University of Oxford, or master of an Academy at Edial, . . . when the greatest men of England were proud to feast him at their table,—still that heavy and remorseful thought came back to him:—'I was cruel to my poor father in his illness!' Many and many a time, awake or in his dreams he seemed to see old Michael Johnson, standing in the dust and confusion of the market-place, and pressing his withered hand to his forehead, as if it ached.
>
> Alas! my dear children, it is a sad thing to have such a thought as this, to bear us company through life." (244)

The moral of this story, given to us in the melodrama of Michael Johnson's "withered hand" pressed to his forehead, is that no possible reparation exists once the moment for immediate and total subjection has passed.

This famous story of Johnson's life held a fascination for Hawthorne:

> The depth and complexity of Hawthorne's filial feelings are revealed by his lengthy involvement with the story of Samuel Johnson's penance in the Uttoxeter marketplace. Repeatedly over a period of twenty-five years he told this story of the great man's compulsion to stand at his deceased father's bookstall at noon before the public gaze. Hawthorne seemed haunted by this image of the aged man of letters choosing public shame in the marketplace to expiate imagined guilt for contributing to his father's death. He recorded this public penance in his notebook in 1838, told it in *Biographical Stories for Children* (published 1842), and recounted his own pilgrimage to Litchfield and Uttoxeter in *Our Old Home*, his last completed work, published in 1863. (Erlich 127)

Gloria Erlich ties Hawthorne's fascination with the Johnson story to "the actual conditions of his childhood and . . . the significance of his troubled relationship to his maternal uncle, Robert Manning": "Hawthorne's equally long period of guilt, confusing a sense of implication in his father's early disappearance and unwitnessed burial with an inability to feel unmixed gratitude for his uncle's benefactions, was not subject to either expiation or resolution. Like Reuben Bourne, he suffered from an obscure sense that the guilt he felt toward his father-surrogate was reciprocal—each had failed the other" (Erlich xiv, 127). Frederick Crews locates Hawthorne's interest in fathers, sons, and their tensions to unresolved Oedipal conflicts. The text of the Johnson story in *Biographical Stories* supports Crews's and Erlich's readings. There is no sympathy for a shy, disfigured boy's reluctance to enter the marketplace. There is an abundance of sympathy for a father who expects his son to brave the public gaze while refusing to aid him toward further maturity by helping him to learn to endure that gaze, by backing his expectations with sympathy and understanding. Instead, Michael Johnson punishes what he sees as Sam's lack of maturity by cursing that lack and thus dooming his son to the lifelong role of disobedient child. Problems of alterity complicate the relations of father and son here. Sam must be enough of an adult to work in public but enough of a child to obey his father; Michael Johnson must raise his child to be an adult. The story can be seen as a narrative meditation on the desire for otherness and sameness in fathers and sons and the tensions such desires create.

When Mr. Temple returns to the story, Johnson is an elderly man in the Uttoxeter marketplace: "His features were scarred and distorted with the scrophula, and though his eyes were dim and bleared, yet there was something of authority and wisdom in his look" (246). Now that he has done penance in the form of lifelong remorse, Johnson can be sympathetically portrayed as an authority figure who has a command over his odd appearance, a public assurance he could not have as a boy. After stressing a list of Johnson's accomplishments, which concludes with, " 'he was now at the summit of literary renown' " (248), Mr. Temple predictably decenters them:

> "But all his fame could not extinguish the bitter remembrance, which had tormented him through life. Never, never, had he forgotten his father's sorrowful and upbraiding look. Never—though the old man's troubles

had been over, so many years—had he forgiven himself for inflicting such a pang upon his heart. And now, in his own old age, he had come hither to do penance, by standing at noon-day in the market-place of Uttoxeter, on the very spot where Michael Johnson had once kept his bookstall. The aged and illustrious man had done what the poor boy refused to do. By thus expressing his deep repentance and humiliation of heart, he hoped to gain peace of conscience, and the forgiveness of God." (248)

Such peace and forgiveness have been missing because of self-denial, not divine denial. Johnson has not forgiven himself, never having shed the guilt over defying his father.

Michael Johnson's curse, which barred repentance, barred divine forgiveness, and insisted upon lifelong guilt, was prompted by a battle in which the young son refused to be subordinate to the aging father. The weight of Johnson's moral domination had to be replaced by something equally weighty once Sam defied domination and realized, if only for a moment, that he could live his life without it. Samuel Johnson's burden of shame and guilt had great significance for him: he carried it constantly and publicly, carried it as a love token of the domination he had lost, the parent he had lost, the child he could never be again. Despite Johnson's real shame and guilt, he can afford repentance and the luxury of guilt and shame because he did refuse his father and thus began his adulthood, and eventually his transformation into Samuel Johnson, man of letters.

Though George and Edward forgive each other once Mr. Temple has made clear the consequences of a continued quarrel, Mr. Temple's narration has not addressed the relationship of brothers. His sons' argument has prompted him to tell a story of father and son, to illustrate that, were their defiance to shift from each other to their father, they would be locked in bondage to their actions, just as Samuel Johnson was locked to his. Michael Johnson was not required—at least not in Mr. Temple's story—to pay in guilt or in shame for the curse he inflicted on his son.

Mr. Temple's story of a father with all the authority and a son with all the guilt should make Edward especially nervous. Johnson's ugliness, near blindness, and disobedience make him, like Edward, an imperfect child. Just as Michael Johnson could not forgive his son's imperfection and so never spoke of Sam's defiance, Mr. Temple has trouble with Edward's physical imperfection and is the only character in the frame stories who never once refers to Edward's blindness. The magic of Johnson's transformation from young boy to ill and aged wizard, from disfigured student to famous scholar, is overpowered by the domination and guilt which flood the sketch. The redefined and reconfigured self is displaced. Hawthorne and the reader, Sam and his father, are instead bound to the world of the actual.

The next story involves another lost son, young Oliver Cromwell, known as little Noll: "'The child was often sent to visit his uncle, who probably found him a troublesome little fellow to take care of. He was forever in mischief, and always running into some danger or other, from which he seemed to escape only by miracle'" (252). Noll is an orphan or at least a bad child, unwanted and so sent away. The absence of any concerned parent is illustrated in the next paragraph, when "'a huge ape, which was kept in the family'" (252), grabs the child and takes him up to the roof. Uncle and ape are surrogate parents for Noll, neither one effectively protecting him from the world's dangers. This scene establishes little Noll as the solitary, alienated figure he will remain throughout the story.

Noll eventually fights with young Prince Charles and emerges victorious. King James, who has brought the prince with him on a visit, cautions his son to avoid temptation "'to tyrannize over the stubborn race of Englishmen'" by remembering "'Noll Cromwell, and his own bloody nose!'" (257). Charles disregards the lesson and lives to be beheaded on Noll's orders. Grown into a man and a leader, Noll is uneasy with his transformation, wondering why "'this great King fell, and that poor Noll Cromwell has gained all the power of the realm'" (259). The only orphan in Mr. Temple's stories, Noll lacks an authority figure who will either bless (as with West's Quaker community) or damn (as with Michael Johnson) his transformation, and so he remains solitary and troubled by his adult success.

When Edward hears the story and gushes, "'Oh, I had rather be blind than be a King!'" Mrs. Temple replies, "'I am glad you are convinced that your own lot is not the hardest in the world'" (260). Her response insists on Edward's resignation to and even gratitude for his affliction. Mrs. Temple's subordinate role in the family circle, her passive listening, and her repeated moralizing suggest that she, too, has learned to occupy the exact amount of space given her and has adjusted to her situation in life, whatever its discomforts may be.

The seventh section of the collection begins with the book's most complete commentary on Edward's blindness, one that implies that the earlier stories have helped Edward on his path to resignation:

> It was a pleasant sight (for those who had eyes) to see how patiently the blinded little boy now submitted to what he had at first deemed an intolerable calamity. The beneficent Creator has not allowed our comfort to depend on the enjoyment of any single sense. Though He has made the world so very beautiful, yet it is possible to be happy without ever beholding the blue sky, or the green and flowery earth, or the kind faces of those whom we love. Thus it appears that all the external beauty of the universe is a free gift from God, over and above what is necessary to our comfort. How grateful, then, should we be to that Divine Benevolence, which showers even superfluous bounties upon us!
>
> One truth, therefore, which Edward's blindness had taught him, was, that his mind and soul could dispense with the assistance of his eyes. Doubtless, however, he would have found this lesson far more difficult to learn, had it not been for the affection of those around him. . . . It taught him how dependent on one another God has ordained us to be; insomuch that all the necessities of mankind should incite them to mutual love.
>
> So Edward loved his friends, and perhaps all the world, better than he ever did before. (261)

Without such happy submission, Edward remains a maimed, miserable child; but with this submission his keepers need not feel uncomfortable around him, since, in his temporary blindness, he is submissive, grateful, and even more loving than before his confinement. This passage relies on sentimentality and the authority of Mr. Temple's stories to guarantee Edward's transformation. The reader is never shown Edward's new happiness, perhaps because Hawthorne himself found it difficult to believe that a small boy could adjust to affliction in a matter of weeks, when an equally uncomfortable man could not adjust in a matter of years.

Like Edward, Ben Franklin, the last male historical figure to be presented, can profit by his misfortunes and the use of his mind's eye. When he sees stones that are to be used in construction on a house, he realizes they are perfect material for building a wharf from which he and his friends can fish and boaters can disembark. " 'Thus, instead of one man, fifty, or a hundred, or a thousand, besides ourselves, may be benefitted by these stones' " (266), he proclaims, envisioning the wharf and its uses.

With stones missing and wharf in evidence, the constable is called, and Ben and his friends are scolded and dismissed. But Ben must still face his father, " 'a sagacious man, and also an inflexibly upright one,' " for whom Ben had " 'greater reverence . . . than for any other person in the world, as well on account of his spotless integrity, as of his practical sense and deep views of things' " (270). Mr. Franklin addresses his son in " 'his customary solemn and weighty tone,' " and Ben feels " 'that now the right and wrong of the whole matter would be made to appear' " (270). Like a caricature of the patriarch, Mr. Franklin is sagacious, upright, deep, solemn, and weighty; his subsequent speech to his son corresponds with his exaggerated character. After explaining that the building of the wharf was misguided and calling the thought behind it impious and destructive, Mr. Franklin concludes: " 'Remember . . . that, whenever we vary from the highest rule of right, just so far we do an injury to the world. It may seem otherwise for the moment; but, both in Time and in Eternity, it will be found so' " (271). Mr. Franklin's reading suggests that actions that seem right can indeed be wrong. In order to avoid error, one must adhere to monolithic orthodoxy or risk offending Time and Eternity.

Such a weighty lesson cannot be dismissed easily, and Ben, like Samuel Johnson, " 'never forgot this conversation with his father; and we have reason to suppose, that, in most of his public and private career, he endeavored to act upon the principles which that good and wise man had then taught him' " (271). With the advice from his father and thus the blessing of the patriarch, Ben can be transformed from young, wharf-building boy to famous American: "'But it would have been a strange dream, indeed, and an incredible one, that should have foretold how great a man he was destined to become'" (272–73). It is debatable whether Franklin did indeed "endeavor to act upon the principles" taught him by his father or whether he continued throughout his life to seek the public good, just as he did in the construction of the wharf. What is clear is that, as in earlier stories, guiltless transformation in *Biographical Stories* is dependent upon the father's blessing on the son.

The frame ends with Mr. Temple telling his audience that *Poor Richard's Almanack* was the reason for Franklin's fame, though the *Almanack* has its deficiencies because the proverbs are "'all about getting money, or saving it'" and "'they teach men but a very small portion of their duties'" (274). Even these seemingly casual comments are weighted with judgment and morality, with a sense of larger contexts and perspectives. Every mention in the book, miscellaneous or significant, seems filtered through a network of rules and disapproval, all judicated by the fathers of *Biographical Stories*.

The last sketch of the collection is markedly different from previous sections. Its historical figure is Christina of Sweden, a rare female among all the male characters, and her story is told in completely negative terms. Earlier stories spotlighted the relationship of father with son, sons who grew up to be famous and admired men;[4] this story centers on a girl whose womanhood is best ignored, "'for it is neither pleasant nor profitable to think of many things that she did, after she grew to be a woman'" (282). The purpose of this tale, paradoxically, is to entertain "quiet little Emily," who "would perhaps be glad to hear the story of a child of her own sex" (275).

Unlike the boys, who learned what they could grow up to be, Emily must learn in negatives and somehow locate herself in the stories of several famous men and one—at least in the eyes of Mr. Temple— infamous woman. Though Emily has been almost silent during earlier stories, Mr. Temple apparently cannot rely upon her silent judgment, for he qualifies his understanding of her potential reaction by saying that she would "perhaps be glad." These early admonitory signs color the story to come with similarities to cautionary tales. Jonathan Cott has pointed to "the excrescence in the seventeenth century of the malignant 'Joyful Deaths' tradition of life-denying Puritan children's books" (3), and collections of English translations of German cautionary tales were equally graphic in showing an extreme punishment always exceeding a transgression at which an adult has first expressed disgust and horror. Thus, in *Struwwelpeter*, a German collection of cautionary rhymes, a boy who sucks his thumbs is first warned and then ("Snip! Snap! Snip! the scissors go") has his thumbs clipped off (16), while in "Queen Christina," a girl who is not taught the eternal feminine virtues not only dies but dies unloved, without " 'a single flower upon her grave' " (283).

At birth, Christina is " 'remarkably plain,' " " 'by no means a beautiful child' " (276).[5] Her lack of beauty matters a great deal to her mother: " 'The Queen, her mother, did not love her so much as she ought; partly, perhaps, on account of Christina's want of beauty; and also because both the King and Queen had wished for a son' " (276). The queen's desire, therefore, was for a son of any physical appearance or, as a distant second choice, a beautiful daughter. Christina's ugliness matters to her mother because Christina, as a female, is a tiny mirror image of her mother and thus should reflect her mother's beauty. From the start, then, Christina and her mother form a sisterhood that is both bound and divided by genetics and gender.[6]

Their struggle is intensified when, as a child, Christina is taken ill. The illness solidifies her relationship with her father, who becomes " 'exceedingly fond' " (276) of her. As the father-daughter bond is cemented, the queen subsides into a permanently peripheral role. Cast as an unloving (wicked) mother from the start, the queen is placed in competition with her daughter for the king's love; when she loses that struggle, she is banished from the story. After the queen's defeat, Christina's socialization becomes even more unorthodox. Having displaced her mother in the king's affections, Christina now becomes a consolidation of the king's desires and is portrayed as a substitute wife as well as a makeshift son.

With the queen in the background, the king determines to educate Christina " 'exactly as if she had been a boy, and to teach her all the knowledge needful to the ruler of a kingdom, and the commander of an army'" (277). Lest the reader have more than a moment to contemplate such an education for a girl, the king's declaration is immediately followed by a narrative admonition: "'But Gustavus should have remembered that Providence had created her to be a woman, and that it was not for him to make a man of her'" (277). The father's blessing on the child's potential transformation is here subordinate to rigid gender boundaries established by Providence or the Nature of Things. Gustavus ignores these boundaries, deriving "'great happiness from his beloved Christina'" (277) as they are shown playing and dancing in the palace. Indeed, Christina's rule over her father is such that "'she could disarm Gustavus of his sword, which was so terrible to the princes of Europe!'" (278). Shown together like father and son, husband and castrating wife, Gustavus and his daughter, Christina, only temporarily avoid the sociosexual consequences of overt defiance of gender and familial restrictions.

When the king is killed in battle, Christina is proclaimed a child queen and separated from her mother. Her growth affected by loss of the same-sex parent (a loss that also affected Hawthorne deeply in his childhood and in his reflections in later years), Christina is isolated from virtues Mr. Temple sees as gender-based. Separated from her mother, Christina is the orphan she appeared to be as a baby, and, without a female model, she continues to pursue inappropriate accomplishments: "'She learned to read the classical authors of Greece and Rome, and became a great admirer of the heroes and poets of old times. Then as for active exercises, she could ride on horseback as well as any man in her kingdom. She was fond of hunting, and could shoot at a mark with wonderful skill. But, dancing was the only feminine accomplishment with which she had any acquaintance'" (281). Though Mr. Temple may categorize dancing as a "feminine accomplishment," Christina's dancing earlier in the story had been portrayed as an enactment of her inappropriate relationship with her father. This somewhat tainted skill was therefore insufficient to sustain her on her journey to womanhood, for Christina "grew up, I am sorry to say, a very unamiable person, ill-tempered, proud, stubborn, and, in short, unfit to make those around her happy, or to be happy herself" (281). As a woman, Christina's first duty, as the sentence indicates, is to "make those around her happy" before she can "be happy herself."

Unlike Christina, other little girls have "'been taught self-control, and a due regard for the rights of others'" (282). Like Clara, her spiritual sister in *The Whole History of Grandfather's Chair*, good little Emily rarely speaks and always listens. The education received from either Grandfather or Mr. Temple imposes a female sense of identity made up of exclusions, because the stories of both feature men only or women negatively. Like Lewis Carroll's White Queen, girls must learn backwards or not at all, and, also like the White Queen, they must adjust to the restrictions of the world: "The White Queen is trying to justify the intolerable, as if she were master of the world and as if the rules were her own invention.... [The White Queen] is in fact inventing the rules, rather as the White Knight invents anklets for warding off sharks, because she is not at all the tyrant in her world, but the victim. The first rule is that there will be punishments; that goes along with 'never jam today'" (Sale 120). Having learned from Mr. Temple's introduction that there will indeed be punishments, Emily must view Christina's behavior as deserving of these punishments. In this way, like the White Queen, she can align herself with those in authority.

Though at age eighteen Christina is "a young woman of striking aspect, a good figure and intelligent face," her eyes reveal "a very fierce and haughty look" (282). This physical evaluation of Christina is almost approving, even if her eyes (which are not bandaged, as Edward Temple's are) hold emotions antithetical to a good and happy woman. Such a favorable description reveals latent sympathy with Christina, showing her as an attractive woman on guard against the world.

But by being born a daughter instead of the desired son, and a plain, sickly daughter at that, Christina had been marked from the start for exclusion from conventional gender categories. As a child she is lost between gender distinctions (a girl raised as a boy), and the gap widens as she ages. Mr. Temple's final emphasis on Christina's personal appearance, once she resigns the throne at age twenty-eight, escapes her enclosures, and devotes herself to traveling, shows her as an antiwoman: "'She is described as wearing a man's vest, a short gray petticoat, embroidered with gold and silver, and a black wig, which was thrust awry upon her head. She wore no gloves, and so seldom washed her hands, that nobody could tell what had been their original color'" (283). Ultimately, despite her knowledge, skills, and throne-resigning independence, Christina must be judged, as she was at birth and at age eighteen, on her appearance. This appearance—masculine, unclean, and ridiculed—is represented as in keeping with Christina's maverick life, as is her death: "'None loved her while she lived, nor regretted her death, nor planted a single flower upon her grave. Happy are the little girls of America, who are brought up quietly and tenderly, at the domestic hearth, and thus become gentle and delicate women! May none of them ever lose the loveliness of their sex, by receiving such an education as that of Queen Christina!'" (283). The exclamatory epitaph for Queen Christina serves as a form of intimidation intended to frighten American girls into delicacy in case the attractions of traditional feminine virtues prove to be an insufficient lure.

In his desire to re-create Christina's place in history solely as a cautionary tale for girls, Mr. Temple's final words return to Christina's education, the catalyst for what he sees as her unfortunate life. Much of his tale, however, has strayed from her education and has stressed that Christina was not gentle, delicate, quiet, tender, or lovely. Mr. Temple wishes that Christina had died rather than had become a woman, especially a woman such as this one. Her birth in plainness marks her as a violation, and she continues, by her very presence, to interfere, to disrupt, and to age, as she displaces her mother in her father's affection, displaces her father as king, displaces various visions of femaleness by her existence. Despite the blame leveled at Christina's education, it is in reality her very existence that Mr. Temple finds disturbing.

"Emily, timid, quiet and sensitive," seems "shocked at the idea of such a bold and masculine character" (283). "With that love of personal neatness, which generally accompanies purity of heart," Emily tells Mrs. Temple that it troubles her "'to think of her unclean hands!'" (283). Emily's only other comment on the story, also directed to Mrs. Temple, is, significantly, "'I never could have loved her'" (283). Emily recognizes another woman, another little girl, and considers responding to her with the love Christina never received in her lifetime and does not receive in this story. But Emily's judgment is limited in that it works only in terms of being good (clean) and being loved; such personal, rather than intellectual, judgment is in keeping with stereotypes of femininity. Emily has not been "spoiled" by an overly intellectual education, as Christina has been; she believes, instinctively, that Christina ought to have pleased those around her by being loveable, that is, clean and neat. Emily's education has been so narrow and ill managed that, finally, she cannot love Christina, because, like Mr. Temple, she believes character is reflected in the cleanliness of one's hands.

Earlier stories in the collection received little more than perfunctory commentary from Mrs. Temple. Christina's story, however, prompts her beyond platitudes. Though she disparages Christina as "'a sad specimen of womankind indeed,'" she also maintains that "'it is very possible for a woman to have a strong mind, and to be fitted for the active business of life, without losing any of her natural delicacy. Perhaps, some time or other, Mr. Temple will tell you a story of such a woman'" (283–84). Perhaps he will, but given the tenor of the story he has just told, it is doubtful, and Mrs. Temple, purposely vague with "perhaps" and "some time or other," is not strong enough to request that story. Emily will have to hear "a story of such a woman" from another woman or create one herself, for Mrs. Temple has not yet learned to be an author and indeed defers the job to her husband. This deference, however, need not be overrated. After all, now that she has heard about Christina's life, Mrs. Temple is able to envision a new sort of biographical story, one that, with its stress on a strong-minded woman "fitted for the active business of life," offers revisionist implications. Too blurry about the edges to begin to tell this story herself, Mrs. Temple has nevertheless progressed on the path to author-ity.

Unlike the other sketches in *Biographical Stories*, Christina's story refuses to allow an authoritative man, a father and a king, to judge what is proper in his child's transformation; Gustavus's wish to educate his daughter as a boy is a transgression that is punished by his death and Christina's monsterhood. It is convenient for the purposes of Hawthorne's story that Gustavus of Sweden was indeed killed during his daughter's youth. Thus, in this version of Christina's life, her

historically accurate orphanhood—father dead, mother banished—
can be used against her, with the implication that she is alone and unloved because she is a plain, masculine, atypical woman, and against
her father, because he was responsible for her miseducation.

The final frame story ends with Edward proclaiming the efficacy
of his inner eye, which again shows him all the main characters of
the stories. He falls asleep and dreams "such a pleasant dream of the
sunshine, and of his dearest friends, that he felt the happier for it, all
the next day. And we hope to find him still happy, when we meet
again" (284). Edward is left happy, though perhaps only temporarily
so, and still enclosed in his darkened room. Edward's happiness is dependent upon his ability to dream, to use his imagination when asleep
or awake. Only when dreaming and using his inner eye is he able to
transform his condition from less than happy to happy. Edward has
moved from being an unhappy, ill child to being a sometimes happy,
ill child.

Since all transformations in the stories are authorized by the father's
reaction, part of Edward's inability to effect a more complete or permanent transformation is due to Mr. Temple's never reacting to his son's
illness. Though Mr. Temple's stories indicate that he believes children
should obey their fathers, the stories tend to tell a different tale when,
for instance, Ben Franklin's disobedience is presented as a reflection of
his thoughtfulness and ingenuity, while Christina's obedience is presented as a reflection of her father's foolishness and her own unnatural
inclinations. As Mr. Temple fails to react to the meaning of his own
stories, stories that attempt to reduce the rich lives of boys and girls
to sterile clichés, he also fails to react to his son's illness and so does
not aid Edward's potential transformation.

Though Hawthorne had the magic to create alternative realities
and transformations in The Whole History, his unwillingness to allow
Edward's metamorphosis in Biographical Stories indicates how uncomfortable he felt with Edward's liminal state—Edward is neither sick
nor well, neither poor nor rich, neither alive nor dead. In Hawthorne's
refusal to allow Edward Temple to move from sick to well or sick to
dying, in his allowing Edward to improve only slightly, Hawthorne
denies his ability to create other realities, denies the art that will af-

ford him only temporary escape. Until Hawthorne himself can escape, Edward must remain as isolated and alienated as his author.

Hawthorne cannot escape in this book, but, like the characters whose lives he portrays, he can invent. He invents *Biographical Stories* and, in so doing, acts out what one of his subjects, Ben Franklin, had learned long ago. Franklin knew that, if one could overcome remnants of guilt about the vanity of authorship, one could invent and that what one invents saves one. By writing *Biographical Stories*, Hawthorne invents, just as all of the characters, Christina included, invent as they transform and thus create themselves. Hawthorne's invention of *Biographical Stories* saves him by allowing him to write his enclosed condition, write his frustration, write his attempt at living his resignation.

Despite the questionable portrayals of women in "Queen Christina," at the time the story was written Hawthorne himself had much in common with the youngest female, little Emily. Like her, he had to locate himself in a world of negatives, a world where a man who worked at the Boston Custom House or wrote for a living did not earn enough money and respect to sustain himself. In such a world, as the White Queen would have known, there were punishments. By creating a narrator such as Mr. Temple and allowing that narrator to condemn Christina, Hawthorne, like little Emily, aligned himself with those in authority, made himself appear as one with the monied, properly employed, unartistic men of the world who seemed to be everything he was not. Indeed, Mr. Temple's harsh treatment of Christina can be seen as a product of Hawthorne's frustration at his own inability to affirm himself as someone eccentric, someone atypical, a creator strong enough to move from alienation and isolation to a declared, defiant identity. In Mr. Temple he externalizes the societally determined figure he feels, guiltily, that he should be.

In his zeal to educate and his temporary, genre-based liberty, Hawthorne was free to give children a strongly biased history lesson, was free to make this lesson angry and full of displaced hostility in order to convey the urgency of his meaning and the frustration of his life. So much more withdrawn than the woman whose history he told, he could not bring himself to admire openly the unconventionality in her that he was reluctant to acknowledge in himself and in his writing. His creation of Mr. Temple to narrate and condemn the problematic course of Christina's life allowed him to mediate his ambivalence toward Christina's social estrangement. Hawthorne's sympathy with Christina in her frustration is demonstrated in his admiration-charged description of her at age eighteen, in his exhaustive catalog of her many accomplishments, and in Mrs. Temple's commentary on the story. After Hawthorne's marriage, after the death of his mother, and after he became a successful author, he sympathetically portrayed women not unlike Christina and greatly diluted the authority of their male narrators or associates.[7] These portrayals were possible once he defied the expectations of society that had chafed him for so long.

By limiting himself to the harsh world of the actual unmediated by the imaginary, Hawthorne denies himself the pleasure of his invention. Instead, he cements the stories of this collection in the world of childhood—perhaps, as Crews and Erlich would have it, the world of his own childhood—where a small figure is forever dominated by a large, mysterious man who controls the world and withholds the possibility of any mediation of the actual. In this setting, Hawthorne cannot escape, as he escaped in *The Whole History of Grandfather's Chair*, because he turns history itself over to the father and allows him to control it, allows him to hammer home again and again—even when the stories themselves belie him—that what history teaches us is that we must do as we are told.

With its combination of genre and subject matter, the last story of this collection aimed at educating his youthful readers educated Hawthorne himself. The history of Christina's life added to Hawthorne's self-knowledge and prepared him, not only for his future portrayals of women and his recognition of their complex role in culture, but also for his own eventual and overdue break from the cultural expectations that had impaired his art and life. In writing *Biographical Stories*, Hawthorne sat in his enclosure, his own form of the darkened room and bandaged eyes, and, like the White Queen, he tried to justify the intolerable. Instead of the White Queen's "never jam today," Hawthorne's justification was his pious and harsh glorification of the restrictions he saw preventing his own transformation from bachelor to husband, from unknown writer to literary figure, from a man who wrote hesitantly and slowly to a confident, inspired artist.

Thematic and epistemological connections built among the tales of this collection hold out hope for the future, show Hawthorne, like Edward Temple, improving slowly, nearly imperceptibly. But, finally, in *Biographical Stories* Hawthorne is savagely refusing himself and the future artists, the future women, in his audience the invention of a world that would allow for the unconventional, that would allow a Christina, a Zenobia, the full possibilities of her biographical story. Hawthorne's action is made all the more savage by his desperate desire to escape his own biographical story.

 **CHAPTER THREE**

The Renewal of Imagination and Faith:
A Wonder Book for Boys and Girls

Ten years after he finished *Biographical Stories*, Hawthorne wrote *A Wonder Book for Boys and Girls*, a collection of six classical myths retold for children, written in six weeks during the summer of 1851, when the Hawthornes lived in Lenox in the Berkshires. *A Wonder Book* was begun scarcely two months after the publication of *The House of the Seven Gables.*

Circumstances favored Hawthorne, the author of two recent and well-received romances, when he wrote *A Wonder Book*. He was in what was to be the most productive period of his literary career; he was a happy, even joyous, husband to Sophia and father to Una, Julian, and newborn Rose; he was temporarily inspired by his natural surroundings; he was a literary figure admired and respected by other authors (including Herman Melville, who lived only six miles away during Hawthorne's stay in Lenox); and he was, finally, the recipient of some fame and financial return from his art. In the midst of such healthy conditions, Hawthorne wrote *A Wonder Book for Boys and Girls*, his most well received and accessible children's book. Reviews at the time were almost unanimously glowing, and critics today who disparage his earlier children's books continue the praise of *A Wonder Book*. Roy Harvey Pearce, who tepidly allows that *True Stories* (*The Whole History* and *Biographical Stories*) "represents Hawthorne's attempts to write for an established juvenile market in an established juvenile genre," rightly calls *A Wonder Book* a product of Hawthorne's "flourishing self-confidence after the success of *The Scarlet Letter* in 1850" (287).

A Wonder Book owes much of its success to elements it shares with the earlier children's works. The structure of frame and sketch seen in *The Whole History* and *Biographical Stories* reappears in a more tightly defined form in *A Wonder Book*. Each tale is divided into three separately titled sections: the first, an "introductory to the story"; the second, the story itself; and the third, "after the story." The frame audience is again composed of children listening to stories, this time narrated by Eustace Bright, a young college student.

In Eustace Bright, Hawthorne presents his youngest narrator of children's stories. Eustace's age bars him from the kind of mature authority manifested by Grandfather and Mr. Temple. For the first time in the children's books, Hawthorne is older, more established, and indeed wiser than his narrator. In *The Whole History* and *Biographical Stories*, Hawthorne (unmarried, childless, financially unsuccessful) was juxtaposed with Grandfather (rich in experience, descendants, and history) and with Mr. Temple (rich in success, paternity, and morality). In *A Wonder Book*, Hawthorne, now himself rich in marriage, paternity, and vocation, creates a narrator who is an undergraduate at Williams College, an aspiring and slightly foolish writer who wants to have his stories published by "Mr. J. T. Fields, . . . [who] will see their uncommon merit, at a glance," and who expects soon to be "reckoned among the lights of the age!" (*A Wonder Book* 170–71). In short, the roles of narrator and author have been transposed, and for the first time Hawthorne clearly has more authority than his narrator. This literary paternity colors the familiar structure of *A Wonder Book* and steadily reveals Hawthorne in comparison and contest with his young narrator.

In addition to its familiar structure, *A Wonder Book* continues the privileging of history and myth. Daniel Hoffman has noted that, in earlier children's works, Hawthorne "mythologizes actual history," while in *A Wonder Book* he "makes mythic actions appear historical" (209). This combination of myth and history, along with Hawthorne's status as "the first writer in English to recast stories out of classical myth for children" (Pearce 311), has resulted in more critical attention for *A Wonder Book*. Most notable among the critical works is Hugo McPherson's *Hawthorne as Mythmaker*, which sees Hawthorne's use of myth "as a vehicle for expressing a personal vision" (108) and usefully compares additions and omissions in the myths of *A Wonder Book* and *Tanglewood Tales* with information given in Charles Anthon's *Classical Dictionary*, Hawthorne's major source for myths. Though Hawthorne would continue his rewriting of myth in *Tanglewood Tales* (1853), the sequel to *A Wonder Book*, in *A Wonder Book* he first turns to myth and returns to children's literature, this time in the flush of success.

Hawthorne's first published rewriting of classical myth for children was indeed in *A Wonder Book*, but he had toyed with the idea as early as 1838 (Pearce 298). When, in 1851, the time and the publisher seemed right, he began to develop his plans. He had written to James T. Fields, his publisher, on April 7, 1851, that he planned the collection to be not "exclusively Fairy tales, but intermixed with stories of real life, and classic myths, modernized, and made funny, and all sorts of tomfoolery" (*Letters* 16: 417). Then, on May 23, again in a letter to Fields, he wrote:

> I mean to write, within six weeks or two months next ensuing, a book of stories, made up of classical myths. The subjects are—The story of Midas, with his golden touch—Pandora's Box—The adventure of Hercules in quest of the Golden Apples—Bellerophon and the Chimaera—Baucis and Philemon—Perseus and Medusa—these, I think, will be enough to make up a volume to be sold at 50 or 75 cts, according to the style of publication. As a frame work, I shall have a young college-student telling these stories to his cousins and brothers and sisters, during his vacations, sometimes at the fireside, sometimes in the woods and dells. Unless I greatly mistake, these old fictions will work up admirably for the purpose; and I shall aim at substituting a tone in some degree Gothic or romantic, or any such tone as may best please myself, instead of the classic coldness, which is as repellant as the touch of marble. (*Letters* 16: 436)

That Hawthorne's plans for the collection were already fairly well developed can be seen in his rejection of "classic coldness" (indicating he had reviewed some version of the classic myths) and in the confidence of his phrase "or any such tone as may best please myself."

He began *A Wonder Book* soon after. Julian Hawthorne recalls that the writing of it was effortless (408), but Hawthorne himself complained to Fields, "It grieves me infinitely to be compelled to write a book, at this season" (*Letters* 16: 443). Both Daniel Hoffman and Nina Baym have described Hawthorne's task in *A Wonder Book* as garnishing or decorating the myths he chose (Hoffman 199; Baym, *Shape* 175), for much of his primary material was borrowed from Anthon. This task, new as it was, combined with Hawthorne's writing in warm weather (an unusual circumstance for him), may have accounted for his complaints. He finished the book quickly, however, and Fields received the manuscript on July 15. Soon afterward, he wrote to his friend Horatio Bridge, "I think it stands a chance of a wide circulation" (*Letters* 16: 461).

Hawthorne's enthusiasm for *A Wonder Book* would remain steady as time passed, and, although it would eventually be surpassed in his affections by *Tanglewood Tales*, *A Wonder Book* merits Hawthorne's fondness. In its pages Hawthorne again transcends the boundaries of time and reaches the mediated world of the actual and the imaginary, a world entered in *The Whole History* and shunned in *Biographical Stories*. His choice of classic myths, teeming as they are with gods in disguise, magic spells, and enchanted objects, immediately locates the stories in the realms of magic and alchemy. The timeless nature of the myths guarantees the full reality of all times and places as Hawthorne approaches them.

In his preface, Hawthorne acknowledges the inherent advantages of the myths, describing them as "marvellously independent of all temporary modes and circumstances. . . . No epoch of time can claim a copyright in these immortal fables. They seem never to have been made" (3). What sets *A Wonder Book* apart from the alternative realities temporarily achieved in *The Whole History* is the ease with which Hawthorne regains that territory, a result of his search, during the years between *Biographical Stories* and *A Wonder Book*, for this place not located on any map, a search concluded in "The Custom House":

"Thus, therefore, the floor of our familiar room has become a neutral
territory, somewhere between the real world and fairy-land, where the
Actual and the Imaginary may meet, and each imbue itself with the
nature of the other" (36). In *The Whole History* Hawthorne gained this
ground only temporarily. By the time he reached "The Custom House,"
he claimed the site as his own, gave its parameters, and fixed it firmly
in his artistic endeavors. In *A Wonder Book*, Hawthorne not only confidently knows the way to this territory, but also, in his relation to his
narrator, reveals his willingness to appropriate stories firmly rooted in
alternative realities. He happily approaches that neutral territory before he begins the actual writing. His choice of narrator (an alternative
to the authority of Grandfather and Mr. Temple) and even his title,
which unabashedly names the predominant good for sale between the
book's covers, reveal Hawthorne's preparation for entrance into the
mediated world of the actual and the imaginary. *A Wonder Book* shows
him entering that neutral territory, not in a desperate desire to escape
reality, not in a violent rejection of the imaginary, not through an
investigation for some way of surviving the Custom House, but as a
familiar, as someone returning home.

The preface to *A Wonder Book* is brief and personal, its tone strong
and decisive. "The author has long been of opinion," (3) it begins, with
Hawthorne putting his opinion first, without apology or equivocation.
His tone, as he comments on his "great freedom of treatment" (3) in
rewriting the myths, continues the opening statement's self-assurance
and reflects Hawthorne's authority: "It will be observed by every one"
(3), he writes, with the certainty that it will be.

His discussion of the myths' timelessness and his rewriting of them
concludes with a refusal to apologize for tampering with "the forms
that have been hallowed by an antiquity of two or three thousand
years" (3). That his discussion does not end in an apology recalls the
preface to the second edition of *The Scarlet Letter* (without, of course,
the gleeful tone of "the author is constrained, therefore, to republish
his introductory sketch without the change of a word") and the preface to *Liberty Tree*, the latter being the only one of the four prefaces
to the earlier children's works that similarly reflects a strong tone and
confident relation with the reading audience. *Liberty Tree*, the third

and last volume of *The Whole History*, benefited from Hawthorne's practice in writing the first two volumes and his relief in beginning the last. The writing and popular success of *The Scarlet Letter* and *The House of the Seven Gables* enabled Hawthorne to make the preface to *A Wonder Book* that much more powerful than its predecessors.

Hawthorne concludes this preface with a revealing explanation of his approach to writing for children:

> In performing this pleasant task—for it has been really a task fit for hot weather, and one of the most agreeable, of a literary kind, which he ever undertook—the Author has not always thought it necessary to write downward, in order to meet the comprehension of children. He has generally suffered the theme to soar, whenever such was its tendency, and when he himself was buoyant enough to follow without an effort. Children possess an unestimated sensibility to whatever is deep or high, in imagination or feeling, so long as it is simple, likewise. It is only the artificial and the complex that bewilders them. (4)

Hawthorne's argument here is not extraordinary; what is notable is the tone of the last two sentences and the fact that they end the preface. Hawthorne tells us what children possess and what bewilders them, brusquely dismisses the opposing viewpoint, and ends the preface. No apology or equivocating tone mars that final sentence. Here Hawthorne knows his audience and has confidence in their acceptance of his authority. This is the striking element in the preface to *A Wonder Book*: Hawthorne finally displays the confidence to recognize, accept, and use the authority granted to him by his knowledge and abilities.

"Tanglewood Porch," the frame of the first sketch, begins with a blanket of "morning mist [that] filled up the whole length and breadth of the valley. . . . It completely hid everything beyond that distance" (5). This mist covers the surrounding landscape, except for "the summit of Monument Mountain" (5) and "the loftier Dome of Taconic" (6). Fiction dissipates the mist and allows one to see the hidden landscape. Each frame story in *A Wonder Book* will include frequent description of landscape, unusual in Hawthorne, and "for which Hawthorne drew from his notebooks" (Baym, *Shape* 174). The notebook entries made during the eight months before Hawthorne began *A Wonder Book* reveal his careful observation of the landscape around him and his temporary affinity for the Berkshires, especially when exploring it in the company of his children.

The children who compose the audience in *A Wonder Book* are named "Primrose, Periwinkle, Sweet Fern, Dandelion, Blue Eye, Clover, Huckleberry, Cowslip, Squash Blossom, Milkweed, Plantain, and Butter-cup; although, to be sure, such titles might better suit a group of fairies than a company of earthly children" (6). The children's names indicate their mostly decorative role as listeners (they do not, for instance, question and comment, as Laurence does in *The Whole History*) and the imaginative personification of their innocence.[1]

The person entrusted with their guardianship when outdoors is "a student at Williams College, and had reached, I think, at this period, the venerable age of eighteen years; so that he felt quite like a grand-father" toward the children (7). Eustace's history is being narrated by Hawthorne himself or by a character Hawthorne has created to represent Nathaniel Hawthorne, author. The earlier children's books strictly limited Hawthorne's overt appearance to the prefaces. Here Hawthorne's authorship is part of the text of *A Wonder Book*. He is no more or less real than Eustace Bright. The idea of authorship is more complex here than it was in *The Whole History* or *Biographical Stories*, where Hawthorne never stepped outside the prefaces to sit at the fire with Grandfather or converse with Mr. Temple. The amused tone con-tinues as he narrates Eustace's history: "His name—(and I shall let you know his real name, because he considers it a great honor to have told the stories that are here to be printed)—his name was Eustace Bright" (6–7). The naming of Eustace, explained by Eustace's unrepressed vanity of authorship, revises Hawthorne's early literary career. No un-signed books or stories will do for Eustace; in his pride, his youth, his foolishness at feeling like a grandfather, Eustace is eager to name himself an author. Hawthorne's recent emergence from his own long wait for fame and recognition allows him to present and poke fun at Eustace's aspirations and pride. By splitting himself off from Eustace Bright, Hawthorne can show the results of vanity of authorship (fool-ishness, pride, vulnerability) and exercise a nearly parental fondness in his acceptance of and generosity toward Eustace and his career. He can afford such a narrator now that his aspirations have been fulfilled and there is no chance that Eustace's hopes as a young writer will be confused with Hawthorne's as a not-so-young writer.

Eustace has "trouble in his eyesight" (7), although, unlike Edward Temple, Eustace's eye problem has done no more than "kept him from college a week or two after the beginning of the term" (7). Hawthorne has "seldom met with a pair of eyes that looked as if they could see farther or better, than those of Eustace Bright," and "a pair of green spectacles" that Eustace wears are "probably, less for the preservation of his eyes, than for the dignity that they imparted to his countenance" (7). The spectacles are immediately snatched off by one of the children and lost in the grass until spring. Ten years after *Biographical Stories*, the locus of author-ity is a young man able to narrate the stories himself, narrate them outdoors (thus without confinement), narrate them without spectacles, and narrate them with pride.

Not only do the children proclaim Eustace's fame as narrator, but Cowslip announces that his stories are "'good to hear at night, because we can dream about them, asleep;—and good in the morning, too, because then we can dream about them, awake'" (8). As Edward Temple knew, happiness depends on one's ability to dream, to use the imagination when asleep or awake. But Edward had to lose his eyesight and work much harder to develop the inner eye that allowed him to transform himself from less than happy to happy, that allowed him to dream while awake. Here, Cowslip, "a child of six years old" (8), has, by listening to Eustace's stories, already learned the lesson so hard won for Edward Temple. The children in the frame scenes of this collection live in a happier, more innocent world than the worlds of *Biographical Stories* and *The Whole History*. No illnesses, no confinements, no squabbles, no stories make them weep; Cowslip and her friends inhabit a sunnier world, a world that is the opposite of the White Queen's. There are no punishments in the seasons that pass in the Berkshire settings of these tales.

In addition to freedom from punishments, there is freedom for Eustace's storytelling from "'old gray-bearded grandsires'" who study the myths "'in musty volumes of Greek, and puzzle themselves with trying to find out when, and how, and for what, they were made'" (9).

Unlike them, Eustace tells the stories by "working up his sophomorical erudition, with a good deal of tact, and incurring great obligations to Professor Anthon," though "he, nevertheless, disregarded all classical authorities, whenever the vagrant audacity of his imagination impelled him to do so" (9). Eustace has the freedom to impose a romantic, a Gothic interpretation on his material and the freedom to ignore traditional interpretation.

Eustace's very lack of experience allows him to disregard classical authorities and shape his art at will. Hawthorne, with more experience, can see too clearly to do this, but as an artist he can create an inexperienced narrator who can transcend the restrictions Hawthorne's own experience imposes on him. Hawthorne differs from his substitution, then, in experience, knowledge, and sight. The substitution of narrators produces artistic freedom and a prelapsarian world where the young narrator is granted unquestioned authority. Together, these elements allow the creation of a sunnier world than Hawthorne could create alone, a world more appropriate for an audience of children.

The story that clears the valley's mists is "The Gorgon's Head," which features Perseus, a valiant and innocent youth; Danae, his unseen mother; and evil King Polydectes, ruler of the island of Seriphus. Polydectes wishes "to do some great mischief to Danae" (11) and to accomplish this sends Perseus to cut off and bring back "'the head of the Gorgon Medusa, with the snaky locks'" (12), and delights in his assumption that Perseus will fail and be turned to stone.

Polydectes wishes to narrate Perseus's life, and he may succeed, because not only must Perseus "fight with and slay this golden-winged, iron-scaled, long-tusked, brazen-clawed, snaky-haired monster, but he must do it with his eyes shut, or, at least, without so much as a glance at the enemy with whom he was contending. Else . . . he would stiffen into stone" (14). Perseus's inexperience is equated with a lack of sight. The task set for him will force him to learn how to see better. As Hawthorne narrates Eustace's experience as a young artist, Eustace narrates Perseus's experience as a novice in the world, a young man incapable of narrating his own story. Both narrators have before them a model that allows for the replication of the self as a more innocent being. Eustace and Perseus are presented without any taint of maturity or experience with the world's cruelties. They receive special treatment from their artist narrators: they never have to pay the price that their culture normally would exact. Perseus leaves and soon meets "a brisk, intelligent, and remarkably shrewd-looking young man" (14), Quicksilver, who volunteers his help and instructs Perseus to polish his shield "'till you can see your face in it as distinctly as in a mirror'" (16). Though Perseus cannot fathom Quicksilver's reasoning, he acquiesces to Quicksilver's authority, which is very like the authority of the artist: he designs a solution to Perseus's troubles, sketches the course of their adventures, and composes Perseus's future experience. Hawthorne narrates a scenario for the young artist that solves all problems of plot and structure by providing a magical, omnipotent character; all obstacles are cleared for the artist's imagination.

Eustace can proceed to solve Perseus's dilemma by composing Perseus's experience around Quicksilver's aid. As Quicksilver magically provides help for Perseus, so Hawthorne magically provides help for Eustace. Hawthorne differs from Eustace Bright in that Eustace is allowed a mentor to aid and teach him. Eustace's narration occurs in a society kinder to the artist, kinder to those, like Perseus, Eustace, and the young Hawthorne, who are trying to learn to control their narrations and to become their own authors. Hawthorne's experience belies the possibility of such a culture, and, in the construct he devises for Eustace, he attempts to preserve the artist from the social neglect that composed his own early experience.

As Perseus prepares to slay the Medusa, he understands "Quicksilver's motive for . . . exhorting him to polish his shield. In its surface, he could safely look at the reflection of the Gorgon's face" (29). In *Home as Found*, Eric Sundquist discusses this moment: "Perseus looks into the shield's mirror in order to see and not to see at once; he perceives the Medusa by a *side-glance*, in the protection of the mirror, and is thus able to sever her head, dealing her the fate that, presumably, she would have figuratively dealt him with a direct gaze" (120). Sundquist pinpoints this moment as a significant one for Perseus: for the first time, Perseus can "see and not see at once." He has indeed learned from Quicksilver. His shield polishing has given him a new way of seeing the world, literally (in enabling him to look at the Medusa) and figuratively (the Greek word *poeta* means "shield polisher"). Now that he has accomplished his task, he has gained experience, proficiency of sight, and the ability to create (*poeta*), to narrate.

When Perseus returns home, the king is "by no means rejoiced to see him" (32). Overcoming his surprise, Polydectes demands the Gorgon's head: "'Pray let me see it!' quoth King Polydectes. 'It must be a very curious spectacle'" (33). Though Polydectes could see earlier that Perseus was an innocent young man, he cannot see now that Perseus could have survived Polydectes' narration of his life only by becoming a narrator himself, by changing the story (death by Medusa) that Polydectes had written for him.

The last page of "The Gorgon's Head" continues the sight puns begun with Polydectes' speech. Though Anthon's version of the myth includes Perseus's showing the head to the crowd, the stress on sight is Hawthorne's addition (McPherson 50). Perseus tells him that the head will "'fix the regards of all who look at it'"; the king's subjects are described as "very fond of sight-seeing"; and, finally, all the island's evil inhabitants gather and "[gaze] eagerly towards Perseus" (33). Perseus feigns reluctance to show the Gorgon's head and in so doing reveals that he is so confident in his narration that he can delay its conclusion. Only when threatened with death does he show the head, thus forcing the islanders to request their deaths at his hand: "And suddenly holding up the head, not an eyelid had time to wink before the wicked King Polydectes, his evil-counsellors, and all his fierce subjects, were no longer anything but the mere images of a monarch and his people. They were all fixed, forever, in the look and attitude of that moment" (34). Now that he can see the islanders for what they are, Perseus can reduce them to images without sight, things that can be seen only.[2] As the story ends, Perseus goes to tell "his dear mother that she need no longer be afraid of the wicked King Polydectes" (34). Perseus now controls not only his own narrative but also his mother's; at the beginning of the story he was incapable of any narration at all.

Like Robin in "My Kinsman, Major Molineux," Perseus begins as an innocent in the world who needs someone to teach him how to read the signs, how thus to avoid disaster. Having promised to perform a seemingly impossible feat contrived to bring about his doom, he leaves the island; he returns capable of gathering the evildoers together and contrives for them to bring about their own doom. Perseus captures the Medusa's head and knows what to do after he captures it. Indeed, once he looks into his shield and understands Quicksilver's instructions, his epistemology suddenly expands: he has been taught to see.

Much of "The Gorgon's Head" hinges on the ability to see and not see, both literally and figuratively. King Polydectes saw Perseus as a fool, but later could not see him as changed, then could not see him at all. Perseus initially could not see the king as evil, but he could after he returned from his journey. The islanders figuratively could never see and eventually can literally see nothing. Again and again, sight is equated with experience. Sight is used in "The Gorgon's Head" to illustrate the movement from blindness, or inexperience, to the ability to "see," to control one's narration, to become one's own author. The successful and experienced narrator can control his own narration and the narrations of others, creating a model for a narrative in which the narrator rules because the narrative is his domain of power. Understanding is dependent on sight: one's understanding can be as misty as the Berkshire valley at the beginning of the frame story or as clear as the day that follows at the end.

Two paragraphs of landscape description end the sketch, some of it drawn from notebooks Hawthorne kept between October 1850 and May 1851. Unlike *The Whole History of Grandfather's Chair* and *Biographical Stories*, the story here is given no further commentary. Instead, we see "rich and diversified . . . autumnal foliage" (36). In *A Wonder Book*, while the myths and their frames are complementary, each has its own province, making the narrative richer and more artistically successful than his earlier children's books.

"Shadow Brook," the next frame, stays with the autumn setting. As the children near a brook whose "dark verdure was changed to gold" (37), they demand a story. Eustace happily complies, because "his mind was in a free and happy state, and took delight in its own activity, and scarcely required any external impulse to set it at work. How different is this spontaneous play of the intellect, from the trained diligence of maturer years, when toil has perhaps grown easy by long habit, and the day's work may have become essential to the day's comfort, although the zest of the matter has bubbled away! This remark, however, is not meant for the children to hear" (39). In the earlier children's books, Hawthorne never compared himself directly to Grandfather or Mr. Temple; here, he points to the difference between the immature storyteller and the mature one. Hawthorne appears to be mourning the loss of "this spontaneous play of the intellect," but he knows, of course, that, while zest brings its own very real rewards, it rarely brings fame, money, or cultural status until it has grown into "trained diligence." The children are not meant to hear this remark, because they are in an experiential void. They will learn in time what boils away with time, as Eustace himself will also learn. Hawthorne offers up to his audience, and perhaps himself, what he has lost in years of writing, what he has endured to reach his present, rather enviable position, what the distance is between his relation to his art now and his relation to it when he was as young, foolish, and spontaneous as Eustace Bright.

Playing on the golden leaves near the brook, Eustace begins King Midas's story in "The Golden Touch," featuring "a little daughter, whom nobody but myself ever heard of, and whose name I either never knew, or have entirely forgotten. . . . I choose to call her Marygold" (40). Bold enough to be filling the myths with new characters and naming them himself, Eustace again shuns a traditional telling of the myths. Eustace's creativity is matched by Hawthorne's, who invents Midas's daughter and the love for her that will transcend Midas's greed (McPherson 56). This new daughter, Marygold (marry gold), has no mother, and King Midas, like King Gustavus in "Queen Christina," loves his daughter more than anything—more, even, than gold itself. Indeed, the two loves become intertwined: "But, the more Midas loved his daughter, the more did he desire and seek for wealth. He thought, foolish man! that the best thing he could possibly do for this dear child, would be, to bequeath her the immensest pile of yellow, glistening coin, that had ever been heaped together since the world was made" (40).

His obsession grows until he must spend each day in his dungeon, surrounded by heaps of gold. He would count coins, sift gold dust, and "look at the funny image of his own face, as reflected in the burnished circumference of the cup—and whisper to himself, 'Oh Midas, rich King Midas, what a happy man art thou!' But it was laughable to see how the image of his face kept grinning at him, out of the polished surface of the cup. It seemed to be aware of his foolish behavior" (42). Midas's image is framed and trapped in the cup, just as he is framed and trapped by his obsession for gold. Though Midas's reflection may reveal the true nature of his behavior, Midas is unaware that his mirror image is any different from how he sees himself, blind as he is to everything but gold and his desire for more of it. Therefore, when a "good-humored and kindly" young man suddenly appears in the dungeon, Midas automatically assumes that "he came to do Midas a favor. And what could that favor be, unless to multiply his heaps of treasure?" (43).

Though the stranger (Bacchus in classical mythology) says his interest is in what would "satisfy" Midas, Midas persists in linking that interest to his own desire for more gold. Impelled by greed, he thinks of "a bright idea. . . . It seemed really as bright as the glistening metal which he loved so much" (44), and he requests a touch of gold. Neither the stranger's broad smile nor his careful questions afterward ("'But are you quite sure that this will satisfy you?'" [44]) alter Midas's reading of an idea that seems as bright as gold.

In the morning he gains the golden touch and turns the contents of his bedroom into gold: "He took up a book from the table. At his first touch, it assumed the appearance of such a splendidly bound and gilt-edged volume, as one often meets with, now-a-days; but, on running his fingers through the leaves, behold! it was a bundle of thin golden plates, in which all the wisdom of the book had grown illegible" (46). Because the book can no longer be read, Midas is denied the knowledge within its pages, knowledge that would have given insight. A few lines later, he turns his spectacles into gold, thus severely limiting his outer vision. Even this does not dismay him, for he reasons, "'The Golden Touch is worth the sacrifice of a pair of spectacles, at least, if not of one's very eyesight. My own eyes will serve for ordinary purposes; and little Marygold will soon be old enough to read to me'" (47).

Midas is shaken, however, when he realizes that food and drink will turn to gold before he can consume them. Once he turns coffee, milk, potatoes, and brook trout into detailed works of gold, he begins "to doubt whether, after all, riches are the one desirable thing in the world, or even the most desirable. But this was only a passing thought" (52). Only when Marygold hugs him and becomes a golden statue is Midas's transformation triggered. He has in effect turned her to stone. As a result, he, too, is transfixed: in his grief, he "could neither bear to look at Marygold, nor yet to look away from her" (53). With his outer vision fixed on her, his inner vision begins to change.

The stranger suddenly reappears, still smiling, and expresses surprise at Midas's misery. Midas declares, "'I would not have given that one small dimple in her chin, for the power of changing this whole big earth into a solid lump of gold!'" (55). The stranger commends Midas's new wisdom and allows him the power of removing the golden touch, which Midas hastens to use. Years afterward, when Midas tells the story to Marygold's children, he maintains, "'Ever since that morning, I have hated the very sight of all . . . gold'" (57). In his wisdom, then, Midas settles on the sight of gold as the source of his trouble. One's desire for gold is determined by whether one sees it with outer sight, inner sight, or some combination of both. For Midas, the sight of gold, commingled with his imaginative view of its powers, caused his obsession; the sight of his daughter as a golden statue transcended his desire and finally allowed his vision to clear.

As Perseus is changed into a wiser man in "The Gorgon's Head," so Midas is changed in "The Golden Touch." Both stories depend upon the intervention of magic initially to complicate and then to resolve events. Both stress sight and who can see in what manner. If one's inner sight is false, one will be in the dark. Both inner and outer vision together must read the signs (Perseus seeing the use of the mirrored shield, Midas seeing Marygold as a statue) before one's sight becomes true.

The story is followed by a paragraph of vivid, enthusiastic description of the surrounding autumn landscape. The warm praise contrasts sharply with the negative account of the Berkshires recorded in his notebook shortly after completing A Wonder Book. Here is the scene as Eustace and the children leave the dell: "The sun was now an hour or two beyond its noontide mark, and filled the great hollow of the valley with its western radiance; so that it seemed to be brimming with mellow light, and to spill it over the surrounding hillsides, like golden wine out of a bowl. It was such a day, that you could not help saying of it—'There never was such a day before!'—although yesterday was just such a day, and tomorrow will be just such another. . . . When the cool night comes, we are conscious of having enjoyed a big armfull of life, since morning" (59–60). This tone, joyous for Hawthorne, would seem to indicate a love for and pleasure in his natural surroundings. Less than three months after he had rhapsodized in this way, he made a surprisingly emotional notebook entry about his surroundings: "This is a horrible, horrible, most hor-ri-ble climate; one knows not, for ten minutes together, whether he is too cool or too warm; but he is always one or the other; and the constant result is a miserable disturbance of the system. I detest it! I detest it!! I de-test it!!! I hate Berkshire with my whole soul, and would joyfully see its mountains laid flat" (*American Notebooks* 439).

This oft-quoted passage, notable for Hawthorne's histrionics, contradicts the landscape descriptions that punctuate the frames of *A Wonder Book*. Yet it was summer when Hawthorne wailed his complaints about Berkshire (a New England season he would not describe in *A Wonder Book*) and, significantly, Sophia was away for two weeks with Una and Rose, leaving Hawthorne, Julian, and Julian's ill-fated pet, Bunny, behind. Though Hawthorne would enjoy time spent with Melville during this period, his notebook entries reveal his unhappiness and anxiety until Sophia's return. For Hawthorne, the presence of his family was inextricably linked to happiness in his surroundings. One of the reasons for the confident and sunny nature of *A Wonder Book* is Hawthorne's family situation as he wrote. Only when they were together could he be fully "conscious of having enjoyed a big armfull of life."

Winter comes and brings Eustace home from college and a blizzard that keeps everyone indoors. The children demand a story to pass the time. In contrast to the wintry scene, Eustace goes back to a time when there was "but one season in the year, and that was the delightful summer; and but one age for mortals—and that was childhood"

(63). Eustace associates the childhood of the world with the childish sensibility of his listeners and the childhood of humankind. Children are therefore the perfect audience for classic myths, because only they possess the sensibility essential to read the signs of tales from the age of myth.

"The Paradise of Children" concerns Pandora's box, which Hawthorne had mentioned briefly, in a notebook jotting in late 1838, as a subject for a fictional piece (Pearce 298). In this version of the Pandora story, children are orphans, and "everybody was a child. There needed no fathers and mothers, to take care of the children; because there was no danger, nor trouble of any kind. . . . It was a very pleasant life indeed" (66). The absence of "those ugly little winged monsters, called Troubles" (66) preserves this childhood of the world and its mortals.

The children in the story are cast as miniature adults playing house together. Pandora comes "from a far country" to live with Epimetheus "and be his playfellow and helpmate" (65). However, the moment she arrives, the surroundings seem less than paradisiacal. Pandora insists upon knowing the contents of a mysterious box left with Epimetheus. Trapped in gender stereotypes, they fight over the box's secret:

> "I am tired of merry times, and don't care if I never have any more," answered our pettish little Pandora. "And, besides, I never do have any! This ugly box! I am so taken up with thinking about it, all the time! I insist upon your telling me what is inside of it."
> "As I have already said, fifty times over, I do not know!" replied Epimetheus, getting a little vexed. "How, then, can I tell you what is inside?"
> "You might open it," said Pandora, looking sideways at Epimetheus, "and then we could see for ourselves." (67)

The sly Edenic request and "sideways" glance invite attention. In "The Gorgon's Head," Perseus "looked sideways" at Quicksilver, "seemed to see wings on the side of his head" (17), and looked sideways at Medusa by looking at her reflection in his shield. Here Pandora's glance shows that she cannot see Epimetheus clearly ("His face expressed so much horror at the idea of looking into a box, which had been confided to him on the condition of his never opening it" [67]) and that she cannot see the box clearly either. As with Midas and his gold, Pandora becomes obsessed with the box, and her sight is distorted by her desire. In trying to see more (by desiring to look into the box), she sees less (by misjudging both her companion and the box's possible contents).

Once the box's lid is lifted, "a crowd of ugly little shapes, with bats' wings, looking abominably spiteful, and armed with terribly long stings in their tails" (76) sting both Pandora and Epimetheus. The two children must suffer the stings of "the whole family of earthly Troubles" (77) and live with the knowledge that "everything, that has since afflicted the souls and bodies of mankind, had been shut up in the mysterious box, and given to Epimetheus and Pandora to be kept safely, in order that the happy children of the world might never be molested by them. Had they been faithful to their trust, all would have gone well. No grown person would ever have been sad, nor any child have had cause to shed a single tear, from that hour until this moment" (77). The release of the troubles causes flowers to begin dying and children to begin aging. The childhood of the world and of humankind has ended due to female desire and distorted sight.

After much bickering, Pandora and Epimetheus together release the last voice in the box. It belongs to Hope, who was "'packed into the box, to make amends to the human race for that swarm of ugly Troubles, which was destined to be let loose among them. Never fear! we shall do pretty well, in spite of them all'" (80). Hope's explanation—that troubles were the world's destiny—partially reprieves Pandora and Epimetheus, and the tale's conclusion is a happy ending to their misbehavior: "And, to tell you the truth, I cannot help being glad. . . . That lovely and lightsome little figure of Hope! What in the world could we do without her? Hope spiritualizes the earth; Hope makes it always new; and, even in the earth's best and brightest aspect, Hope shows it to be only the shadow of an infinite bliss, hereafter!" (81). The now mortal children in the former paradise are happier than before the box was opened. Despite their transformation and their subsequent vulnerability to the effects of troubles, they now see their former paradise as "the earth's best and brightest aspect," limited by its lack of promise of later "infinite bliss."

Hawthorne's retelling of the Pandora myth is a "growing-up story, a child's version of the Paradox of the Fortunate Fall" (Pearce 308), which in this case is the result of Pandora's greed and selfishness. Epimetheus "had his own share of curiosity" about the box, and "we must not forget to shake our heads" at him as well as Pandora (75–76). Yet Pandora bears the burden of guilt in the text: before her arrival, the box is safe and all is peaceful. She makes the box her obsession, corrupts Epimetheus, and lifts the lid. Her portrayal as a representative female is extended to the story's female audience: "She felt just as anxious to take a peep, as any of these little girls, here around me, would have felt. And, possibly, a little more so;—but of that, I am not quite so certain" (71–72). Her behavior is explained as gender-specific, and the story's female audience is thereby implicated in the fall. Epimetheus has misbehaved, but Pandora, alas, has been true to her nature.

Unlike Midas, her spiritual father, Pandora has no opportunity to redeem herself and see more clearly. Her lack of opportunity is a condition of this young world: "It might have been better for Pandora if she had had a little work to do, or anything to employ her mind upon, so as not to be so constantly thinking of this one subject. But children led so easy a life, before any Troubles came into the world, that they had really a great deal too much leisure. . . . When life is all sport, toil is the real play" (70). As Daniel Hoffman has pointed out, "Hawthorne cannot conceive of the Golden Age without foreboding" (201). That foreboding, however, is linked to traditional gender definitions. The reduction in characters' ages and therefore their desexualization are Hawthorne's construct, not Anthon's (McPherson 59), but it is not a successful strategy to free them from gender codes. In their desexualization and leisure, they are still subject to the official machinery regulating sociosexual relations. Pandora and Epimetheus both are trapped within patriarchal scripts, beyond which they cannot see to other ways for expressing themselves. The release of Hope and the promise of later "infinite bliss" is, then, an improvement, a move forward. The world and the children will age, but they can now "hope" for "infinite bliss" to come in a new world, perhaps one that will allow the children to realize their full possibilities.

The children in the Tanglewood playroom are also left happy. Their privileged lives in Tanglewood allow them to believe that childhood will be pleasant and eternal—that there is, in fact, "but one age for mortals." Their childish community encourages this belief: "Had there been only one child at the window of Tanglewood, gazing at this wintry prospect, it would perhaps have made him sad. But half-a-dozen children . . . may defy old Winter" (83). At least in the happier and possibility-filled world of this collection, these children will avoid the negative effects of winter, age, and gender stereotypes.

A few days after the snowstorm in "Tanglewood Fireside," the next introduction, Primrose tells Eustace, " 'The children have talked so much about your stories, that my father wishes to hear one of them, in order to judge whether they are likely to do any mischief' " (87). Eustace resists the prospect of an adult auditor—Mr. Pringle, Primrose's father—who wishes to evaluate and judge his narrations and authorship. He explains his resistance on the grounds of age, aesthetics, and knowledge: " 'Besides, your father is a classical scholar; not that I am much afraid of his scholarship, neither, for I doubt not it is as rusty as an old case-knife, by this time. But then he will be sure to quarrel with the admirable nonsense that I put into these stories, out of my own head, and which makes the great charm of the matter for children, like yourself. No man of fifty, who has read the classical myths in his youth, can possibly understand my merit as a re-inventor and improver of them' " (87–88). Eustace mentions and then disparages Mr. Pringle's classicism, age, and knowledge of classical myths read in his youth. That Hawthorne himself is forty-eight years old (nearly a "man of fifty") when he writes A Wonder Book is a half-concealed joke that points again to the difference between Hawthorne and his narrator and allows Hawthorne to associate himself both with Mr. Pringle, his contemporary, and with Eustace Bright, a rewriting of his younger self.

Eustace is the representative of romanticism, and Mr. Pringle, the voice of classicism, ready to censure Eustace's liberties with the myths as "likely to do . . . mischief." When Eustace enters the drawing room, tall, handsome Mr. Pringle turns to him "in a way that made him feel how uncombed and unbrushed he was, and how uncombed and unbrushed, likewise, were his mind and thoughts" (89). Mr. Pringle's thoughts, grooming, and attire are conventionally—indeed, classically—determined. Eustace is one of those messy romantics, so his thoughts, grooming, and attire likewise represent his position on the margins of culture and his concern with convention, whether in the tailoring of clothes or in interpretations. A younger Hawthorne facing his Puritan ancestors, Eustace has nothing but stories to recommend him. Like Hawthorne, he may quail, but he continues his authorship: "'If you will find patience,'" he tells Mr. Pringle after some preliminary murmurs about Mr. Pringle's lack of sympathy, "'I will find stories'" (89). For the first time in the children's books, a narrator is confronted by a critical, culturally empowered adult listener. Grandfather's audience was composed solely of children; Mr. Temple's, of children and Mrs. Temple. Now that he has gained a measure of authority himself, Hawthorne can afford to create such a model.

Perhaps due to Mr. Pringle's presence, the story that Eustace tells, "The Three Golden Apples," is the weakest story in *A Wonder Book*. Despite the misleading title, the story concerns Hercules' adventures as he seeks the apples in fulfillment of his eleventh labor. Not the apples but the quest for them is significant, for "it was quite a common thing with young persons, when tired of too much peace and rest, to go in search of the garden of the Hesperides" (91), where the apples grow. As in the golden age in "The Paradise of Children," too much leisure leads to trouble.

The restless hero of "The Three Golden Apples" has "enjoyed very little peace or rest, since he came into the world" (91), and now searches for a famous garden, a fruitless search until he locates the Old Man of the Sea. Once found, the old man changes into a stag, a seabird, a dog, a monster, and a snake, all in an attempt to frighten Hercules away. "These magical transformations" fail to dismay Hercules, who can "see the difference between real dangers and imaginary ones," which is "one of the hardest things in this world" (100). Since Hercules' inner and outer sight are coordinated and correct, he sees the old man for what he is, no matter what he appears to be at any given time. Because Hercules has inner sight, magic does not blind him, and he receives the information he needs. Anthon's article on Hercules is long, and Hawthorne therefore had many incidents from which to choose (McPherson 63). That he chose to include the old man's transformations reveals his affinity for scenes invoking the real and the imaginary.

Hercules arrives "on the shore of the great ocean" and uses "an immense cup or bowl . . . ten times larger than a great mill-wheel" to cross the ocean to the garden of the Hesperides (102): "Accordingly, without a moment's delay, he clambered over the brim, and slid down on the inside, where, spreading out his lion's skin, he proceeded to take a little repose. He had scarcely rested, until now, since he bade farewell to the damsels on the margin of the river. The waves dashed, with a pleasant and ringing sound, against the circumference of the hollow cup; it rocked lightly to-and-fro; and the motion was so soothing, that it speedily rocked Hercules into an agreeable slumber" (103). After this nap in the golden, womblike cup, Hercules wakes and sees "a giant, as tall as a mountain; so vast a giant, that the clouds rested about his midst, like a girdle, and hung like a hoary beard from his chin" (103–4). Atlas, supporting the sky in his hands, tells Hercules that only he can go to the Hesperides and gather the golden apples and adds, " 'Were it not for this little business of holding up the sky, I would make half-a-dozen steps across the sea, and get them for you' " (105–6). Though Hercules was able to see the Old Man of the Sea as he was, he cannot see Atlas as he is, and so Hercules agrees to hold up the sky while Atlas gets the apples. Hercules is blinded by both his "kind heart" in allowing Atlas a rest and his resulting vanity "if he could boast of upholding the sky" (106).

When Atlas returns with the apples, he refuses to take the sky back, telling Hercules that it will do his reputation good to continue: declares Atlas, " 'posterity will talk of you, I warrant it!' " (109). Being able to boast of upholding the sky no longer attracts Hercules, who responds, " 'Pish! A fig for its talk!' " (109). Now that he can see Atlas for who he really is, he slyly asks the Titan to take the sky back for a moment, while he makes a cushion of his lion's skin for the weight to rest upon. Atlas complies, whereupon Hercules seizes the apples "and straightway set[s] out on his journey homeward, without paying the slightest heed to the thundering tones of the giant, who bellowed after him to come back" (110). Hercules refuses, and "to this day," says the narrator, when we hear rumbling thunder "we may imagine it to be the voice of Giant Atlas, bellowing after Hercules!" (110).

On this Irvingesque image "The Three Golden Apples" ends, the apples having appeared only briefly and the garden of the Hesperides having never been glimpsed. Despite his adventures, Hercules has not altered; despite his slumber in the golden cup, he has not been reborn. At the story's end, he strides off, as driven and unsatisfied as ever. Images familiar in earlier children's stories—a quest, a golden age, sight, magical transformations—have appeared here, yet they are complicated by Hercules' relentless dissatisfaction, the unresolved nature of the text, and the near absence of apples and garden. The romantic and classical have met in Eustace and Mr. Pringle, and the resulting narration resists analysis. Though artistically unsuccessful, "The Three Golden Apples" is interesting as Hawthorne's narrative positing of what sort of text would result when the romantic and classical struggled.

Mr. Pringle, "after some deliberation," delivers his typically dismissive critical judgment: "'I find it impossible to express such an opinion of this story as will be likely to gratify, in the smallest degree, your pride of authorship. Pray let me advise you never more to meddle with a classical myth. Your imagination is altogether Gothic, and will inevitably gothicise everything that you touch'" (112). Mr. Pringle attacks Eustace's use of the Gothic, but Eustace is allowed a clear, simple, and knowledgeable defense: "'And, Sir, if you would only bring your mind into such a relation with these fables, as is necessary, in order to re-model them, you would see at once that an Old Greek has no more exclusive right to them, than a modern Yankee has. They are the common property of the world, and of all time. The ancient poets re-modelled them at pleasure, and held them plastic in their hands; and why should they not be plastic in my hands as well?'

"Mr. Pringle could not forbear a smile" (112). After his story, Eustace is not made to look foolish in front of Mr. Pringle. Though Mr. Pringle dislikes Eustace's treatment of myth, he bows to Eustace's defense. As Nina Baym has pointed out, "Eustace and his host clash entirely on aesthetic grounds. The artist has a place in this comfortable, satisfied, tolerant, commonsense world of the American gentry. . . . Half patronized and half patron, he is a member of the family. He can talk back to authority" (*Shape* 176). Now that Hawthorne has his own place in the world as an artist, he can afford to create a young, fledgling artist who can respond when challenged. This world is kinder than the one in which Hawthorne the young artist found himself, and this change is reflected in Mr. Pringle's limited appearance in *A Wonder Book* (he appears only in the introductory and concluding frames of "The Three Golden Apples"). The aesthetic argument between Eustace and Mr. Pringle is not further detailed. Though their confrontation is rich in binary oppositions (young/old, unconventional/traditional, artistic/critical), it is limited. Hawthorne locates his emphasis elsewhere and avoids justifications of validity in the text.

In the next frame, Eustace, home for his spring vacation, looks "pretty much as we saw him, four or five months ago, except that, if you gazed quite closely at his upper lip, you could discern the funniest little bit of a moustache upon it. Setting aside this mark of mature manhood, you might have considered Cousin Eustace just as much a boy, as when you first became acquainted with him" (115–16). The growth of spring has brought the growth of Eustace, but such minor growth that one needs to "gaze quite closely." Mocking his narrator's young manhood, Hawthorne asks his young readers to laugh with him. In the frame stories, Eustace is repeatedly portrayed as an awkward child pretending to be a man, and Hawthorne repeatedly pokes fun at Eustace's signs of adulthood. Nearly fifty years old, with his marriage, his children, and his success as his credentials into manhood and authority, Hawthorne can finally narrate Eustace's awkward young manhood from a safe distance.

Ironically, Eustace goes on to tell a story of old age and domestic happiness in "The Miraculous Pitcher." Philemon and Baucis, an elderly couple, are the only hospitable inhabitants of a village characterized by meanness to travelers. The two sit outside their cottage, listening to "the rude shouts of children and the fierce barking of dogs, in the village near at hand" (118), and they realize the villagers have turned the dogs on a stranger. Philemon shakes his head and prophetically remarks, "'I should not wonder if some terrible thing were to happen to all the people in the village, unless they mend their manners'" (118–19). Philemon and Baucis, known for their kindness, "felt as if . . . guests had a sort of holiness, and that they ought therefore to treat them better and more bountifully than their own selves" (119).

Pursued by dogs and children, the two travelers, a young man and an older man, appear, "disdaining to notice either the naughty children or the pack of curs" (121). Baucis prepares the strangers a meal, and Philemon notices that the young man is dressed "in rather an odd way" (123). Again, Quicksilver's appearance (for it is he) causes others to question their sight: Philemon, whose "eyesight was none of the sharpest" (123) and "whose eyes, you know, were getting rather dim" (123), has trouble discerning where the strangeness of his visitor lies. The elderly traveler, less odd in appearance, asks about the villagers and "looked so stern, that Philemon was really almost frightened" (124), especially when, as the older man frowns, the twilight deepens and thunder rumbles overhead. Though able to see goodness in all people, Philemon cannot see the real identities of Jupiter and Quicksilver. Their magic both invites (by the oddities of their appearance and behavior) and defies (by their disguises) outer sight.

This obfuscation of outer sight continues during the meal the travelers are served. When the pitcher is empty yet continues to pour milk, Baucis "could scarcely believe her eyes" (128). Though she empties it, she can see "as plainly as she could see anything" (129) that more milk remains. The bread, the honey, and the grapes are likewise multiplied, and Philemon, doubting Baucis's surprise, checks the pitcher "to see into it with his own eyes" (131). Though it is empty when he looks, it fills when Quicksilver pours from it. Baucis and Philemon clearly see the transformations of the food, but they dare not trust their outer sight, even though they never distrust their inner sight.

As the strangers prepare to leave the next morning, Philemon and Baucis see that the village has disappeared under a lake. The elderly traveler explains the fate of the villagers: "'There was neither use nor beauty in such a life as theirs; for they never softened or sweetened the hard lot of mortality by the exercise of kindly affections, between man and man'" (135). Turned into fish, their neighbors have literally become the "'scaly set of rascals, and the coldest-blooded beings'" (135), that were in life. Jupiter stands as an Old Testament God, associated with loaves, fishes, and destruction. For their kindness, the couple is offered a wish, and they request to "'leave the world at the same instant, when we die!'" (135–36). Jupiter grants their wish, transforms their cottage into a palace, and makes the milk pitcher permanently enchanted.

After many years, Philemon and Baucis disappear, and in their place appear "two venerable trees" with boughs "intertwined together, and embraced, . . . so that each tree seemed to live in the other tree's bosom, much more than in its own" (136, 137). Even though they could not believe their eyes when they initially saw transformations, in the end Philemon and Baucis are likewise changed. Hawthorne's version of the myth corresponds closely with Anthon's (McPherson 69). The major additions are the sight references and the deep affection of Philemon and Baucis. In Hawthorne's version, Philemon and Baucis's love causes them to love the world and to see goodness in all people. That inner sight is more valuable than being able to read enchanted milk pitchers. Philemon and Baucis, in Hawthorne's reading, are blessed and divinely subsumed into each other and the natural world.

This portrait of an aging and loving couple suggests Hawthorne's happiness in his marriage to Sophia, a happiness revealed in his journal entries throughout their marriage, though perhaps particularly so in the Berkshire period. During Sophia's two-week absence a few months after *A Wonder Book* was completed, Hawthorne wrote in his notebook, using Sophia's pet name: "God bless me, for Phoebe's and all their sakes! No other man has so good a wife. . . . Would I were worthier of her. . . . My evenings are all dreary, alone, and without books that I am in the mood to read; and this evening was like the rest. So I went to bed about nine, and longed for Phoebe" (*American Notebooks* 473).

Two days earlier, Hawthorne and Julian had gone on a day trip to a Shaker village with Melville and Evert and George Duyckinck. They had spent the day rambling to such a contented end that, after his company had left, Hawthorne wrote, "It was a most beautiful night, with full, rich, cloudless moonlight, so that I would rather have ridden the six miles to Pittsfield, than have gone to bed" (468). Two days later

Hawthorne was sadly bemoaning Sophia's absence. Though his outing was enjoyable, though the moonlight and the company were tempting, the impulse was a temporary one, unlike his need for the stable and secure family situation that likewise kept him stable, secure, and happy. This relationship and need underlie the whole of A Wonder Book and inform the loving relationship of Baucis and Philemon in "The Miraculous Pitcher."

"Bald Summit," the introduction to the final tale, again takes place in the spring, this time as Eustace and the children climb a nearby hill. In demanding a story, Primrose says, "'Now that we are up among the clouds, we can believe anything!'" (143). Eustace fixes "his eyes on a white cloud that was sailing by" (143), revealing that his storytelling is as spontaneous as ever, that he is therefore still nearly a child himself, and begins "The Chimaera," the final tale of A Wonder Book.

The story begins as Bellerophon arrives at the Fountain of Pirene, enchanted bridle in hand, and asks a middle-aged man, an old man, a young woman, and a little boy if they "'know whether the winged horse Pegasus still haunts the Fountain of Pirene, as he used to do'" (145). The replies are not encouraging. The middle-aged man jeers, asking, "'Of what use would wings be to a horse?'" and concluding, "'No, no! I don't believe in Pegasus. There never was such a ridiculous kind of a horse-fowl made!'" (147). The old man says, "'[I] used to believe there was such a horse. . . . But, now-a-days, I hardly know what to think. . . . And, to tell you the truth, I doubt whether I ever did see him'" (147). The young woman thinks she may have heard Pegasus neigh once, but the sound frightened her away.

The child, Bellerophon's last hope, has seen the winged horse, though only when he looks "'down into the water'" can he see "'the image of the winged horse, in the picture of the sky that is there'" (148). A direct glance, he explains, alerts the horse, who then flies away. Unlike the middle-aged man and the old man, the child believes his eyes and imagination. Therefore, "Bellerophon put his faith in the child, who had seen the image of Pegasus in the water, and in the maiden, who had heard him neigh so melodiously, rather than in the middle-aged clown who believed only in cart-horses, or in the old man, who had forgotten the beautiful things of his youth" (148).

Faith rests with a child who knows that the horse, like Medusa, can be seen only indirectly, only by a sideways glance. The main elements of this version of the myth are Anthon's (McPherson 71); the stresses on sight, faith, and imagination are Hawthorne's additions.

Bellerophon watches for Pegasus, is mocked by "rustic people," and is supported by "the gentle child," who often looked "down into the fountain and up towards the sky, with so innocent a faith that Bellerophon could not help feeling encouraged" (149). Unlike the adults in the story, the child has not learned through experience to doubt his sight of winged horses. Bellerophon is empowered by the child's pure imagination. This image of the "childish visionary" (Baym, *Shape* 178) partakes of Victorian sentimentalizing of children, and the child is emblematic of Bellerophon's own imagination.

Bellerophon wishes to use the horse to slay the Chimaera and thereby "make all mankind admire and love him" (150). Like Eustace's hopes in storytelling and Hawthorne's in writing, Bellerophon's hopes are for success, and, also like them, he must wait. Indeed, waiting taxes Bellerophon the most: "Oh, how heavily passes the time, while an adventurous youth is yearning to do his part in life, and to gather in the harvest of his renown! How hard a lesson it is, to wait! Our life is brief; and how much of it is spent in teaching us only this!" (152). Hawthorne's sympathetic aside is for Bellerophon waiting at the fountain, Eustace waiting at Williams College, and Hawthorne's younger self waiting in Salem, waiting in the Custom House, waiting for his life to change. Now that Hawthorne has passed out of life's waiting room, he sympathizes with those who remain behind. Bellerophon, like Hawthorne, is left with only his imagination to sustain him, for "if it had not been for the little boy's unwavering faith, Bellerophon would have given up all hope" (152). That faith in imagination serves him well.

Pegasus appears and is as beautiful as the child promised. Powerful, winged, wild, and male, Pegasus is a revision of the woman whose death gave him life: "created from the blood of Medusa's decapitated head," Pegasus is "thus mythically linked with female power and female inspiration" (Gilbert and Gubar 529). In "The Gorgon's Head," Medusa had to die before Perseus could have any power; in "The Chimaera," Pegasus, fueled by female power though born a male, lives as Bellerophon's eventual loving partner.

Once Bellerophon has seen Pegasus, his task, though still difficult, becomes possible and no longer requires the steady presence of imagination to support it. Leaping on Pegasus's back, Bellerophon flies to Helicon Mountain, thwarting the horse's attempts to dislodge him. Pegasus is magically tamed, though virtually enslaved. The product of imagination and faith, the object of Bellerophon's greatest desire, Pegasus is a dream come to life. But that dream, if enslaved, Bellerophon realizes, is not his ideal, and so he releases Pegasus. The horse at first flies away but then returns and grows fond of Bellerophon.

Bound together by love and friendship (the result of Bellerophon's faith and imagination in attempting to fulfill his desire), they fight the Chimaera, "the ugliest and most poisonous creature, and the strangest and unaccountablest, and the hardest to fight with, and the most difficult to run away from, that ever came out of the earth's inside" (150). At the conclusion of their difficult battle, the Chimaera attaches itself to Pegasus, who is ridden by Bellerophon, and they sail with it "higher, higher, higher, above the mountain-peaks, above the clouds, and almost out of sight of the solid earth" (164–65). Only in this position, much closer than at any previous point in the battle, is Bellerophon able to slay the Chimaera: "Perhaps, after all, the best way to fight a Chimaera is by getting as close to it as you can" (165). The Chimaera symbolizes Bellerophon's greatest fear, just as the gentle child symbolized his imagination and Pegasus symbolized his realized dreams.

After the battle, Pegasus and Bellerophon return to the Fountain of Pirene, where they find "the country fellow," "the old man," and "the pretty maiden" (166). All three respond characteristically to the sight of Pegasus: the country fellow wishes to clip his wings and turn him into a cart horse, the old man remembers him as lovelier, and the young woman runs away in fear. Unable to achieve any combination of the actual and the imaginary, they cannot perceive either. Because of the circumscribed nature of their vision, they exist in a closed world and are unable to expand their vocabulary of signs. This is the world that awaits those who lose faith and imagination, who cannot wait long enough to see their dreams realized.

The gentle child appears, weeping with joy at Bellerophon's victory. Bellerophon and Pegasus fly off together, and the story ends with the prophecy that the child, "gentle and tender as he was, grew to be a mighty Poet!" (167). It is fitting that the boy, symbol of the flight and power of imagination, transforms himself into an artist. The last character seen in the retold myths is one whose sight has needed no adjustment.

In the final frame section, Hawthorne praises the treatment of the Pegasus story, saying that Eustace "had contrived to breathe through it the ardor, the generous hope, and the imaginative enterprise of youth" (168). This final editorial comment stresses the symbolism of "The Chimaera" and points again to the commingling of Eustace's age and art. Eustace proclaims that, were he to have Pegasus at Tanglewood:

> "I would mount him, forthwith, and gallop about the country, within a circumference of a few miles, making literary calls on my brother-authors. Dr. Dewey would be within my reach, at the foot of Taconic. In Stockbridge, yonder, is Mr. James, conspicuous to all the world on his mountain-pile of history and romance. Longfellow, I believe, is not yet at the Ox-bow; else the winged horse would neigh at the sight of him. But, here in Lenox, I should find our most truthful novelist, who has made the scenery and life of Berkshire all her own. On the hither side of Pittsfield sits Herman Melville, shaping out the gigantic conception of his 'White Whale,' while the gigantic shape of Graylock looms upon him from his study-window. Another bound of my flying steed would bring me to the door of Holmes, whom I mention last, because Pegasus would certainly unseat me, the next minute, and claim the poet as his rider." (169)

In his biography of Melville, Edwin Haviland Miller has pointed to this "graceful allusion" to Melville in A Wonder Book and Melville's dedication of Pierre to "Greylock's Most Excellent Majesty" (250). While certainly graceful, Hawthorne's reference has none of the admiration of Melville's dedication to Moby-Dick ("IN TOKEN OF MY ADMIRATION FOR HIS GENIUS, This Book is Inscribed TO NATHANIEL HAW-

THORNE"); indeed, it is more reserved and less familiar than its brother references in the same passage. Much has been written about Hawthorne and Melville's parting after the neighborly summer of 1851; the publication of *A Wonder Book* has its small role to play in this parting. In October, when Hawthorne wrote to his publishers and enclosed a list of names of those who were to receive advance copies of *A Wonder Book*, Melville's name was not among them (*American Notebooks* 699). Instead, the eldest Melville child received from Hawthorne a copy of *A Wonder Book* inscribed, in Melville's handwriting, "Master Malcolm Melville from Mr. Hawthorne Nov: 7th 1851" (Sealts 66). The nature of this inscription indicates Melville's knowledge of the gift and desire to record the source. Hawthorne may have given the book in this manner in order to reconfirm his friendship and respect for Melville or perhaps to remind the ardent Melville of their mutual status as fathers, as husbands, as men attached to their families. In this passage of *A Wonder Book*, Hawthorne's narrative strategy allows him to use Eustace to talk about Melville, just as he will use Malcolm Melville when the book is published.

At the end of the frame section, Primrose asks about another neighborhood author " 'whom we sometimes meet, with two children at his side, in the woods or at the lake. I think I have heard of his having written a poem, or a romance, or an arithmetic, or a school-history, or some other kind of a book' " (169). As in the facetious introduction to "Rappaccini's Daughter," Hawthorne mocks himself in this list of his accomplishments. However, here he concludes with a warning from Eustace that acknowledges the magic power of Hawthorne as author: " 'Something whispers me that he has a terrible power over ourselves, extending to nothing short of annihilation' " (170). Full of confidence that allows him to mock his accomplishments as motley and to transform himself into a god with complete power over his creations, Hawthorne ends *A Wonder Book*. Eustace maintains that his stories will soon be published, and the children and Eustace "made the best of their way home to Tanglewood" (171).

We are left with Hawthorne's self-portrait as a father and as a writer of some power, power enough to annihilate. Hawthorne can afford to mock his writings and reputation as motley precisely because they are no longer so. He is freely and happily mocking what he once feared he was, not what he—and the world—now know him to be.

The golden age Hawthorne depicted in *A Wonder Book for Boys and Girls* has its parallel in the golden age that he felt he was then living in Lenox. His personal golden age, "a time outside of time, a living eternity" (Hoffman 201), encompassed his happiness with Sophia, his freedom from past worries about his art and potential success, and his fondness for and delight in his children, beloved companions who saw the world as new. The steady company of children allowed Hawthorne, too, to see the world as new. In *A Wonder Book* he multiplied their presence to include the children in the audience he addresses, the children in the frame stories, his own children (to whom he read the stories as he wrote them), and Eustace Bright, his child narrator.

Committed as he was to preserving the full reality of all times and places in the pages of *A Wonder Book*, Hawthorne was therefore also committed to a narrator who could freely enter the childish world of the myths. This commitment required a narrator almost a child himself and allowed Hawthorne domination and paternity over him. Like Quicksilver gently mocking Philemon and Baucis's efforts to see, Hawthorne mocks Eustace's efforts to grow beyond his youth, to see his way into adulthood and art. As Quicksilver manipulates events for Perseus, Pandora, Epimetheus, Philemon, and Baucis, so Hawthorne manipulates events for Eustace, placing Mr. Pringle in his path, allowing him to grow a moustache, trumpeting his hopes of publication, and chiding him for his inexperience in the world. While Eustace grounds the stories in the golden age of childhood, Quicksilver and Hawthorne, in the stories and the frames, hover over that world and design the events that happen within it. As artists, they have full control over their creations, and their playfulness masks their ability to annihilate.

Such manipulation in *A Wonder Book* does not lead to the same lessons found in *The Whole History* and *Biographical Stories*. Where Grandfather's stories did not swerve from impressing the children with a sense of the horror and wrongs of the past, and where Mr. Temple's stories warned his children of the many ways they could be brought to misery, Eustace's stories do not stress any knowledge of suffering. Eustace's inexperience allows him to tell stories in a way that Grandfather and Mr. Temple, because of their experience, could not. Eustace's narration in *A Wonder Book* is Hawthorne's passport to a world not sagging under the weight of painful experience—a world of and for children. For the adult, this innocent childhood "could be remembered, recovered in the imagination, so as to serve as a measure of what the adult had lost and what he had gained" (Pearce 306). Unlike the lessons of *The Whole History* or *Biographical Stories*, then, *A Wonder Book*'s lessons avoid tragic knowledge and encourage knowledge that allows for growth and learning within childhood.

This view of children's literature results in stories that are intended to expand the epistemology of the characters and the audience. Character after character, from Perseus to Bellerophon, goes through experiences that teach the importance of coordinating outer sight (controlled by the eyes) with inner sight (controlled by the imagination). When such fine tuning is achieved, a marriage of the actual and the imaginary comes about and one can defeat one's enemies, solve one's problems, achieve one's fondest desires, and gain a permanent and life-sustaining faith in one's ability to read and understand the world around one. Such experience will eventually lead one to knowledge of suffering and thus into adulthood. But as this is preferable to death (the only alternative to adulthood), it is best that the stories prepare one to understand Grandfather's lessons of the past and Mr. Temple's morals, that they teach one how to see, how to discern, how to cherish one's imagination and faith.

Not only does Hawthorne write *A Wonder Book* from that neutral territory "somewhere between the real world and fairy-land, where the Actual and the Imaginary may meet, and each imbue itself with the nature of the other," not only does he wish always to write from that place—he wishes always to understand the world from that place. Such a desire suggests the authority Hawthorne gained from his success in what he saw as fierce cultural competition and from his mastery of the imaginative space that inspired his artistic discourse. If this neutral territory can be gained not only in art but in life, then every day becomes a day out of the golden age: every day allows for the possibility of a winged, white horse emerging whole and unstained from a pool of blood; every day becomes for us—as readers, as children, as adults—a day out of the everyday life of Nathaniel Hawthorne when he lived in the Berkshires and wrote out his wishes in *A Wonder Book for Boys and Girls*.

CHAPTER FOUR

The Loss of Hope: *Tanglewood Tales*

anglewood Tales, written in early 1853, is the last book of fiction Hawthorne completed in America and his final children's
book. Written two years after *A Wonder Book for Boys and Girls*
as a sequel to that collection, it is by no means the sunny and happy
work that *A Wonder Book* is proclaimed to be. Though both books
are retellings of Greek myths and are written for children, *Tanglewood
Tales* is complicated by a less carefully crafted structure, images of
death and loss, and sanitized and coded sexual relationships. *Tanglewood Tales* was as financially and critically well received as *A Wonder
Book*, but it is nonetheless less artistically successful and, all in all, a
more troubled and problematic text.

Much had happened to Hawthorne during the months that inter-
vened between his writing of the two books: the Hawthornes had
moved across the state from Lenox to Concord; Hawthorne's sister,
Louisa, on her way to visit them, had drowned in July 1852; Sophia's
mother had died in early 1853; pre–Civil War rumblings were becoming increasingly difficult to ignore; Hawthorne's friendship with
Herman Melville, at its peak during the writing of *A Wonder Book*, no
longer colored his daily life; and, despite Hawthorne's growing fame
as a writer, it was increasingly clear that his writing would provide,
at best, a slender means of existence. Such events challenged Hawthorne's worldview, and it is no wonder that *Tanglewood Tales* shares
little of its predecessor's form, approach, or content.

Unlike *A Wonder Book*, *Tanglewood Tales* has no introduction and conclusion to each tale and no conclusion to the completed work. It consists only of the introduction and the six tales. Eustace Bright functions as no more than the token narrator. He appears in the brief introduction, holds a literary conversation with Hawthorne, is somewhat patronizingly dismissed, and then is neither seen nor mentioned again. Eustace's absence has prompted Nina Baym to conclude: "The author of the stories in *Tanglewood Tales* is not after all the unsophisticated Eustace but the older, disenchanted Hawthorne. Apparently, the adult problems he thought to escape by retelling classical myths for children returned to him in these very myths—which, after all, are not tales for children" (*Shape* 214). The events of Hawthorne's life caused him to stagger under the burden of his life's history, to begin to lose his faith. A long-lost father; a newly lost sister; two lost mothers; a lost friendship; the lost innocence of his growing children; the loss of his belief in the possibility of artistic success, cultural approbation, and adequate financial return; the loss of the promise seen in America: all combined to shake Hawthorne's deep-rooted faith in the possibility of gaining experience without being destroyed.

Tanglewood Tales stands as Hawthorne's last effort to convince himself that things had not changed as radically as it seemed, that one could gain knowledge and experience without losing faith. That his attempt to renew his faith takes place in a children's book is fitting. He had always seen children as a pure and innocent audience, as humankind made new, as symbols of hope and faith for the experienced: "Hawthorne's insistent belief, one which runs through virtually all of his writing, [is] that childhood is that period of life in which innocence, directness, and clarity are paramount facts. It was a period that had inevitably to be left behind once the child entered upon the tragic rigors of adulthood. Yet it could be remembered, recovered in the imagination, so as to serve as a measure of what the adult had lost and what he had gained" (Pearce 306). In *Tanglewood Tales*, Hawthorne looks to this audience for the buoyancy that he had once found there, looks to find what he "had lost and what he had gained."

Hawthorne therefore approaches *Tanglewood Tales* and his imagined neutral ground "somewhere between the real world and fairy-land,

where the Actual and the Imaginary may meet, and each imbue itself
with the nature of the other," with altered experience, sensibility, and
vision. In his maturity, then, his attitude toward literature for children
has changed. In discussing Hawthorne's earlier view of literature for
children, Baym has written:

> Literature for the child must be *purely* imaginative in that it has no
> human substance to work on, is therefore directed away from reality
> rather than toward it. The imagination here does not enrich reality by
> fuller awareness of it—as Thoreau and Emerson defined imagination—
> but rather seeks to escape reality by reaching, like Poe, toward a super-
> nal world. Unlike Poe, however, the child as Hawthorne sketches him is
> incapable of conceiving of fear or horror; part of its inexperience is the
> total absence of pain from its world. ("Hawthorne's Myths" 41)

In *Tanglewood Tales*, "the child as Hawthorne sketches him" is certainly capable "of conceiving of fear or horror," because the events
of the child's life are composed of just that. Like Poe, Hawthorne
reaches toward a supernal world that embraces fear and horror as
part of the childhood experience. In his confidence with the written
word and in the maturity of his authorship, Hawthorne writes tales of
irrevocable loss.

Not only has his conception of literature for children changed, his
purpose in addressing such an audience has also changed: "Consider
the probable intent of *Grandfather's Chair*: to inculcate a positive ap-
preciation of democratic values without erecting the 'Americanism' of
the 1830's and 1840's into an exhaustive standard of value" (Colacurcio 645). Hawthorne has moved beyond the limited expression of
nationalism as a vehicle for understanding time itself to a vision of the
psychological landscape, a vision so primary, so basic to our fears of
the world, that it is embedded in classic myth.

Written at a crucial point in Hawthorne's literary career, *Tanglewood
Tales* (1853) follows immediately after *The Scarlet Letter* (1850), *The
House of the Seven Gables* (1851), and *The Blithedale Romance* (1852).
Last in line after the three major romances, *Tanglewood Tales* is a cru-
cible for the talent that fueled the major works. As such, *Tanglewood
Tales* colors current critical understandings of the trajectory of Haw-

thorne's literary career. An examination of the collection allows for a reenvisioning of this trajectory, a reenvisioning of this life.

Hawthorne finished the book in March and sailed for England in July. *Tanglewood Tales* was published in his absence in August. "He wrote Richard Henry Stoddard, March 16, 1853, shortly after finishing *Tanglewood Tales*, 'I never did anything else so well as these old baby stories'" (Pearce 311).[1] Despite this show of confidence only days after finishing the manuscript, Hawthorne never again attempted to express his faith in children or, indeed, to express his faith in himself by approaching an audience that had so readily lent itself to the creation of alternative realities.

In "The Wayside," the introduction to *Tanglewood Tales*, Hawthorne, while speaking with Eustace, uses the summerhouse on his property as a trope for the classical myths: "'The summer-house itself, so airy and so broken, is like one of those old tales, imperfectly remembered; and these living branches of the Baldwin apple-tree, thrusting themselves so rudely in, are like your unwarrantable interpolations'" (177). His tone recalls Mr. Pringle's to Eustace in *A Wonder Book*, and, indeed, the literary discussion that follows plays upon the roles of the old (Hawthorne the older writer, formerly Mr. Pringle) and the new (Eustace the writer, formerly Eustace the storyteller):

> It will be remembered, that Mr. Bright condescended to avail himself of my literary experience by constituting me editor of the Wonder Book. As he had no reason to complain of the reception of that erudite work, by the public, he was now disposed to retain me in a similar position, with respect to the present volume, which he entitled "Tanglewood Tales." Not, as Eustace hinted, that there was any real necessity for my services as introductor, inasmuch as his own name had become established, in some good degree of favor, with the literary world. But the connection with myself, he was kind enough to say, had been highly agreeable; nor was he by any means desirous, as most people are, of kicking away the ladder that had perhaps helped him to reach his present elevation. My young friend was willing, in short, that the fresh verdure of his growing reputation should spread over my straggling, and half-naked boughs; even as I have sometimes thought of training a vine, with its broad leafiness and purple fruitage, over the worm-eaten posts and rafters of

the rustic summer-house. I was not insensible to the advantages of his proposal, and gladly assured him of my acceptance. (178)

Hawthorne's implication that Eustace is now, in literary reputation, superior to Hawthorne himself centers on the issue of age. Eustace is young, Hawthorne old; Eustace is fresh, Hawthorne worm-eaten; Eustace's reputation is growing, Hawthorne's straggling and half-naked. Hawthorne, in comparing himself with the model of the young artist, sees himself as worn out by age, weakened by time, unable to transcend temporal limits.

His review of Eustace's manuscript reveals that his opinion of classic myth has also changed substantially. He wonders how Eustace "could have obviated all the difficulties in the way of rendering them [the myths] presentable to children. These old legends, so brimming over with everything that is most abhorrent to our Christianized moral-sense—some of them so hideous—others so melancholy and miserable, amid which the Greek Tragedians sought their themes, and moulded them into the sternest forms of grief that ever the world saw;—was such material the stuff that children's playthings should be made of! How were they to be purified? How was the blessed sunshine to be thrown into them?" (178–79). This oft-noted passage points to artistic complexities in the re-creation of the myths that were not engaged earlier. In A Wonder Book, the myths at their worst were beautiful but "cold and heartless" (112–13). The myths as Hawthorne now sees them are abhorrent, hideous, melancholy, and miserable. They offend the morals and invite readers into "the sternest forms of grief." Eustace criticized the myths in A Wonder Book, but Hawthorne recoils from them in Tanglewood Tales.

Hawthorne's doubts do not appear as dialogue in the text. Eustace's response is likewise related indirectly, this time by Hawthorne. Both the rhetorical avoidance of direct dialogue and Hawthorne's role as mediator between Eustace's response and the reader suggest internal dialogue, an argument that the artist is having with himself:

But Eustace told me that these myths were the most singular things in the world, and that he was invariably astonished, whenever he began to relate one, by the readiness with which it adapted itself to the child-ish purity of his auditors. The objectionable characteristics seem to be a parasitical growth, having no essential connection with the original fable. They fall away, and are thought of no more, the instant he puts his imagination in sympathy with the innocent little circle, whose wide-open eyes are fixed so eagerly upon him. Thus the stories (not by any strained effort of the narrator's, but in harmony with their inherent germ) transform themselves, and re-assume the shapes which they might be supposed to possess in the pure childhood of the world. When the first poet or romancer told these marvellous legends (such is Eustace Bright's opinion) it was still the Golden Age. Evil had never yet existed; and sorrow, misfortune, crime, were mere shadows which the mind fan-cifully created for itself, as a shelter against too sunny realities—or, at most, but prophetic dreams, to which the dreamer himself did not yield a waking credence. Children are now the only representatives of the men and women of that happy era; and therefore it is that we must raise the intellect and fancy to the level of childhood, in order to re-create the original myths. (179)

Hawthorne views childhood in general as a re-creation of the child-hood of humankind. This construct allows him to glorify the purity of childhood and to place Eustace (and thus Eustace's conjectures on the nature of the myths) somewhere between childhood and adult-hood. In "Eustace's" reading of the myths, "the sternest forms of grief" become shadows or "at most, but prophetic dreams": the perspective of the youthful artist allows him to disempower the world's woes.

Hawthorne dismisses Eustace's earnest, paragraph-long defense, condescendingly choosing to "let the youthful author talk, as much and as extravagantly as he pleased, . . . glad to see him commenc-ing life with such confidence in himself and his performances. A few years will do all that is necessary towards showing him the truth, in both respects" (179–80). "Youthful" authors talk and perform extrava-gantly, have confidence in themselves and their work. Age, according to Hawthorne, will shake the confidence in both and render Eustace like Hawthorne: without confidence in self or work. Eustace's praise of childhood "must be qualified by the inexperience of the youthful Eustace. A mere college student, he has not yet crossed the threshold of his own life into the realm of responsible action" (Hoffman 200). If time must teach him, then Eustace himself is still a member of the golden age. Eustace's role is limited in *Tanglewood Tales* because he is young, inexperienced, and therefore innocent. The artist who had a place in *A Wonder Book* has no place, familial or otherwise, in the experienced world of *Tanglewood Tales*. This experienced world needs an experienced author. Eustace does not yet meet this requirement and so his appearance in *Tanglewood Tales* is brief and truncated.

Hawthorne's next inquiry concerns the children in *A Wonder Book*'s frame stories. He learns that "Primrose is now almost a young lady"; "Periwinkle is very much grown"; and "Sweet Fern has learned to read and write, and has put on a jacket and pair of pantaloons—all of which improvements I am sorry for" (180–81). The children's "improvements" show signs of growth and age. As such, they begin to take the children beyond childhood to the world of sorrow and adulthood. Young as they are, they are no longer the innocents of *A Wonder Book*.

Eustace, too, has grown. He is now in his last year at Williams College. Hawthorne sees Eustace on the threshold of a career choice, as Hawthorne himself was in his last year at Bowdoin: "I do not know what he means to do with himself, after leaving college, but trust that, by dabbling so early with the dangerous and seductive business of authorship, he will not be tempted to become an author by profession. If so, I shall be very sorry for the little that I have had to do with the matter, in encouraging these first beginnings" (181). Early dabbling in a "dangerous and seductive business" would seem to enhance its attraction. Hawthorne's description does not imply that time lessens the seduction and danger. His reservations stem from the meager financial rewards and precarious position in life offered by authorship. Eustace, once he has grown, will be no more fit for material paucity than Hawthorne found himself to be in early 1853.

The introduction's final paragraph is Hawthorne's fond farewell to his young audience. Because we know that the introduction was written by Hawthorne after he finished the myths (Pearce 309), his farewell strikes a plaintive note: "I wish there were any likelihood of my soon seeing Primrose, Periwinkle, Dandelion, Sweet Fern, Clover, Plantain, Huckleberry, Milkweed, Cowslip, Butter-cup, Blue Eye, and

Squash Blossom, again. But as I do not know when I shall re-visit Tanglewood, and as Eustace Bright probably will not ask me to edit a third Wonder Book, the public of little folks must not expect to hear any more about those dear children, from me. Heaven bless them, and everybody else, whether grown people or children!" (181–82). Hawthorne's litany of the names of all the children in *A Wonder Book*'s frame stories ends with no hope of seeing these children again, because soon they will be children no more. There will be no more children, no more Eustace, no more of Hawthorne's books for children. Hawthorne's qualified statement that there will be no more news of the children "from me" stresses his inability to continue his former discourse with this audience.

His final blessing to the world remains as a cry for a blessing upon himself. Forced by his experience and sensibility to know and feel too much sorrow and misfortune, forced by his nature to write that sorrow and misfortune, Hawthorne needs this blessing to mediate his experience. Thus, with the blessing of heaven on reader and writer, the nightmare world that is *Tanglewood Tales* begins.

"The Minotaur," the first story in the collection, opens with a boy named Theseus, his mother, Aethra, and a mythical, distant father: "As for his father, the boy had never seen him. But, from his earliest remembrance, Aethra used to go with little Theseus into a wood, and sit down upon a moss-grown rock, which was deeply sunken into the earth. Here she often talked with her son about his father, and said that he was called Aegeus, and that he was a great king, and ruled over Attica, and dwelt at Athens" (183). When Theseus asks for his father, Aethra answers that his "'father will never be able to leave his kingdom, for the sake of seeing his little boy'" (183). From the start, Theseus is in a typically Hawthornean situation. Gloria C. Erlich's discussion of *The Scarlet Letter* stresses this model: "Although such mothers as Hawthorne depicted in his works are clearly mothers, fathers are represented in diffuse and fragmented ways. . . . Maternal presence and paternal absence are the positive and negative poles that generate this historical romance. . . . The absence of a father becomes the dominant question for the community, the clergy, the governor, and most of all for the child" (27). As persistent in his search for his father as Pearl is for hers, Theseus asks why he cannot "'go to this famous city of Athens, and tell King Aegeus that [he is] his son'" (184). Aethra tells him that when he is able to lift a certain heavy stone he may then journey to Athens. She is "sorrowful" at the idea of his eventual growth and departure. Her desire to extend his childhood conflicts with her patriarchal narrations that encourage Theseus's attempts against the boulder.

The passage of childhood is marked by his lifting of the stone. His joy is his mother's grief: "He looked joyfully at his mother; and she smiled upon him through her tears" (186). Beneath the rock, Theseus finds "a sword, with a golden hilt, and a pair of sandals" (186) left by his father: "'That was your father's sword,' said Aethra, 'and those were his sandals. When he went to be King of Athens, he bade me treat you as a child, until you should prove yourself a man by lifting this heavy stone. That task being accomplished, you are to put on his sandals, in order to follow in your father's footsteps, and to gird on his sword, so that you may fight giants and dragons, as King Aegeus did in his youth'" (186–87). Aethra is suddenly revealed as more caretaker than parent. Aegeus's orders have defined the limits of Theseus's childhood, just as stories about Aegeus have dominated Theseus's imagination. Though Aethra has been physically present, Theseus's childhood has been determined by his absent father.

Theseus leaves Aethra for Athens. When his cousins and his father's wife, Medea, hear of him, they plot his death before infirm King Aegeus can learn his identity. Aegeus recognizes Theseus, and the plot fails. Medea, Aegeus's wife and so a wicked stepmother to Theseus, flees in "her fiery chariot" drawn by "four huge winged serpents, wriggling and twisting in the air" (194). Theseus displaces Medea just as Aegeus displaced Aethra. Wife and mother—women good or evil—have no place in the world of the father and son.

Theseus now leads an idyllic life with his father, paralleling his childhood with his mother. This pastoral stage ends when Theseus wakes to "sobs, and groans, and screams of woe, mingled with deep, quiet sighs" (196) of human sacrifices fated for the Minotaur. Like other monsters in *A Wonder Book* and *Tanglewood Tales*, the Minotaur symbolizes a challenge to be met and defeated. Despite his father's dismay, Theseus volunteers to be one of the sacrifices. Aegeus left Aethra and Theseus; Theseus left Aethra; now Theseus leaves Aegeus. Weak Theseus once longed for his father. Now weak Aegeus must long as his son sacrifices himself for power, enough power to become the father he once desired so desperately.

Father and son agree that, if Theseus triumphs, the ship's black sails will be changed to those "'bright as the sunshine'" for the return voyage (198). Aegeus's sight of the bright sails and his final sight of his son as Theseus sails away are pictures out of Hawthorne's ancestry, the generations of Hathorne men (the spelling of the family name before Hawthorne changed it) who, like Hawthorne's father, went to sea. In this sea parting, however, the roles are reversed: the son sails away, leaving the weaker father behind.

The ship reaches Crete, and Theseus exchanges proud words with King Minos. In his evil kingship, Minos is the dark half of King Aegeus, a father to be defeated. Minos's daughter, Ariadne, betrays her father and takes Theseus to the maze the night before his ordeal. She holds one end of a thread, gives him the other, and, with her encouragement, he enters the maze to find and fight the Minotaur. With thread in hand and Ariadne on the other end, Theseus need not fear losing himself in the maze: "He would have felt quite lost, and utterly hopeless of ever again walking in a straight path, if, every little while, he had not been conscious of a gentle twitch at the silken cord. Then he knew that the tender-hearted Ariadne was still holding the other end, and that she was fearing for him, and hoping for him, and giving him just as much of her sympathy as if she were close by his side. Oh, indeed, I can assure you, there was a vast deal of human sympathy running along that slender thread of silk!" (206–7). In *A Wonder Book*, Pandora and Epimetheus were desexualized by age reduction; here the connection between Ariadne and Theseus is desexualized by sentimental rhetoric: "gentle twitch," "tender-hearted," "Oh, indeed, I can assure you." This rhetorical strategy is undercut by the "sexually charged" nature of these images in Freudian terms (McPherson 83).

Ariadne's power, sexual or not, is peculiar and significant. She can help Theseus triumph, but she cannot triumph herself: "Ariadne alone has the clue that will thread a way through the labyrinth and the fact that she is still unable to effect her own escape make[s] her an important symbol . . . of female helplessness and the resilience, supportiveness, and endurance such helplessness paradoxically engenders" (Gilbert and Gubar 527). For Theseus, she symbolizes female nurturance. She is another woman, like Aethra, who will give to him while taking nothing for herself because to give is her purpose.

Theseus meets the Minotaur and as they begin to fight, the Minotaur, assembling sounds into language, "belched forth a tremendous roar, in which there was something like the words of human language, but all disjointed and shaken to pieces by passing through the gullet of a miserably enraged brute" (208). The Minotaur fails to communicate his rage in language; Theseus communicates his in fighting skill. He attacks the Minotaur, separating the bull's head from the man's body, the otherness from the human. In defiance of two fathers, with the aid of a mother, Theseus has reached the center of a maze where he kills a primitive, male, inarticulate voice of rage. Like Bellerophon killing the Chimaera, the symbol of his greatest fear, Theseus kills the animal rage of his own mazelike depths.

Led by a triumphant Theseus, the other human sacrifices flee after the killing. In this version of the myth, Theseus begs Ariadne to escape with him, while she nobly refuses to desert her father: "Now, some low-minded people, who pretend to tell the story of Theseus and Ariadne, have the face to say that this royal and honorable maiden did really flee away, under cover of the night, with the young stranger whose life she had preserved. They say, too, that Prince Theseus (who would have died, sooner than wrong the meanest creature in the world) ungratefully deserted Ariadne, on a solitary island, where the vessel touched on its voyage to Athens" (210). This revision putatively improves the false and low-minded version told by others. Yet the revision itself lies repeatedly: the "honorable maiden" betrayed her father, Theseus did "wrong the meanest creature" by slaughtering the Minotaur, and adult readers know the false reading to be the true one. Eustace earlier asserted that "childish purity" banished the myths' "objectionable characteristics" so that they "re-assume[d] the shapes which they might be supposed to possess in the pure childhood of the world" (179). But here the objectionable qualities remain, the myth is untransformed. This is not re-vision, a new way of seeing, but denial, implying that there is no other truth here but the one we fear to acknowledge.

The group sets sail, and, "amidst the sports, dancing, and other merriment" (211–12), Theseus neglects to alter the ship's black sails. This "sad misfortune" leads to Aegeus's death (211): "No sooner did he behold the fatal blackness of the sails, then he concluded that his dear son, whom he loved so much, and felt so proud of, had been eaten by the Minotaur. He could not bear the thought of living any longer; so, first flinging his crown and sceptre into the sea, (useless baubles that they were to him, now!) King Aegeus merely stooped forward, and fell headlong over the cliff, and was drowned, poor soul, in the waves that foamed at its base!" (212). The sight of the black sails triggers Aegeus's suicide; the son's sea voyage results in the loss of the father by drowning. In Charles Anthon's *Classical Dictionary*, Hawthorne's source for the myths, Aegeus "destroyed himself" (qtd. in McPherson 80); Aegeus's death by drowning is Hawthorne's detail.

This is a tale of loss: father, then mother, then father again; evil parent figures; raging monsters; helpless yet powerful women; sea voyages; drowning and suicide. In the writing of *A Wonder Book*—a scant eighteen months earlier—Hawthorne had no need to read the signs of "the sternest forms of grief," his inner voices had no need for the powerful release derived from the rendering of tales so "melancholy and miserable" (179).

Theseus's search for his father ends with his father's death. Theseus assumes the throne and his father's role. Aethra joins Theseus, and mother and son end the story as they began it. The crucial difference is the absence of Aegeus—in stories, instructions, and physical presence—to determine Theseus's life. Once the center of that life, Aegeus has been the father to worship, to leave, to forget, and finally to displace. Hawthorne's lighthearted ending to "The Minotaur" denies the tale's contents, a denial that resounds through each of the six myths in *Tanglewood Tales*.

In the next tale, "The Pygmies," the giant Antaeus is the father figure to a pygmy tribe "six or eight inches" tall, living in "little cities, with streets two or three feet wide, paved with the smallest pebbles, and bordered by habitations about as big as a squirrel's cage" (213). Antaeus—one-eyed, friendly, good-natured, dull-witted—co-exists happily with the tribe, the latter priding themselves on his superior strength and size.

This friendship is interrupted by Hercules, who stumbles upon the community and is challenged by Antaeus. Hercules defeats Antaeus, tosses his corpse away, and naps in exhaustion, unaware that the pygmies, enraged at the death of Antaeus, are gathering about him. They attack Hercules, but their violent efforts succeed only in waking him and his sense of humor at the futility of their attack. In a fit of laughter—"'Ha, Ha, Ha! Ho, Ho, Ho! For once, Hercules acknowledges himself vanquished!'" (233)—Hercules strides away, leaving the pygmies without their former friend and mentor, Antaeus, and with only a hollow victory to avenge his death.

Just as Ariadne and Theseus's traditional parting was challenged as a falsehood, so, too, is this traditional ending, which Anthon included in his article on the pygmies (McPherson 85):

> Some writers say, that Hercules gathered up the whole race of Pygmies in his lion's skin, and carried them home to Greece, for the children of King Eurystheus to play with. But this is a mistake. He left them, one and all, within their own territory, where, for aught I can tell, their descendants are alive, to the present day . . . reading their little histories of ancient times. In those histories, perhaps, it stands recorded, that, a great many centuries ago, the valiant Pygmies avenged the death of the giant Antaeus, by scaring away the mighty Hercules! (233)

If the pygmies' "little histories" are as nationalistic as some histories of American events, then, instead of recording a weak and futile response to devastating loss, they would trumpet the attack of Hercules as triumphant revenge for Antaeus's death. Hawthorne's revision of the myth's ending attempts to shift narrative attention from the heavy presence of Antaeus's corpse by looking to the pygmies' future and glorifying the actions of their ancestors. The description, "a great many centuries ago," does distance the reader from Antaeus's death, but not enough to obscure the dead father, not enough to obscure the small, powerless pygmies watching their lives irrevocably altered by the father's choice (Antaeus's challenge to Hercules) and defeat, not enough to obscure the structure of a tale that sets up a family relationship only to knock it down.

More familial loss occurs in "The Dragon's Teeth," when Europa, sister of Cadmus, Phoenix, and Cilix and playmate of Thasus, is carried off by "a snow-white bull" while her playmates chase a butterfly (235). The bull entices Europa onto his back and then plunges into the sea; neither he nor Europa are ever seen again. In his rage at the abduction of his daughter, King Agenor orders his sons to find Europa or never return. In a matter of moments, then, the sons lose their sister and their father. Queen Telephassa, their mother, grieved by Europa's loss, chooses to accompany them and so loses her husband as well as her daughter.

Telephassa, her three sons, and Thasus set off in search of Europa, and thus begins the pilgrimage that is "The Dragon's Teeth." As the pilgrimage wears on, one by one they abandon the search, settle, and form and rule communities. Phoenix settles first, saying, "'Our sister is lost, and never will be found. She probably perished in the sea'" (242). That Europa is "lost" is supported by the lack of traces after her disappearance. Her absence is worse than her death would have been because she cannot be located in memory as a completed life and so is lost permanently to her loved ones. Phoenix's conjecture that his sister has been lost through an unwitnessed drowning recalls King Aegeus's drowning, Hawthorne's father's unwitnessed drowning, and the more recent drowning of Hawthorne's own sister, Louisa. Here, indeed, the actual and the imaginary have met and blended. The imaginative ground of "The Dragon's Teeth" allows Hawthorne to establish a mode of discourse in which he can write about sudden, permanent loss.

Cilix drops out next, telling his companions, "'We are like people in a dream! There is no substance in the life which we are leading'" (244). He, too, settles and is made a king. His kingship, like the kingships of the other settlers, gives him power and status but not enough to displace the ontological crisis of Europa's abduction. Europa's loss comes to represent their figurative loss of innocence; they begin to read the world differently ("like people in a dream") yet are unable to

forget completely how they read it before. This epistemological alteration causes them to question the shape and values of their former
lives. As their experience changed (and as Hawthorne's experience
changed), so their worldview, their concerns, and their very perception of reality altered radically. They must come to terms with this
alteration, their understanding taking the form of a literal journey,
Hawthorne's taking the form of fiction.

Thasus departs next, leaving Telephassa and Cadmus, the two remaining pilgrims, behind. They continue, querying strangers who,
noting Telephassa's mad behavior, advise Cadmus " 'to get this dream
out of her fancy,' " to which he replies, " 'It is no dream! . . . Everything
else is a dream, save that!' " (248). Mother and son are equally obsessed by the pilgrimage; his vision of reality has become as distorted
as hers. The act of searching, not its goal (the finding of Europa), has
become their focus; permanent loss is their obsession.

Telephassa dies, advising Cadmus in her final words to consult the
oracle of Delphi for advice. He does so and hears "a rushing sound, or
a noise like a long sigh, . . . [which] began to sound like articulate language. It repeated, over and over again, the following sentence, which,
after all, was so like the vague whistle of a blast of air, that Cadmus
really did not quite know whether it meant anything, or not:—'Seek
her no more! Seek her no more! Seek her no more!' " (251). Like
the Minotaur's bellowing, the sounds are close to language, but ultimately they are only partially understood. If the Delphic oracle, a
source of wisdom, is nearly as unreadable as the Minotaur's howl, then
the unintelligible bellow recalls the wisdom of the ages. Communica-
tion, or understanding, then, is determined by the speaker's ability to
avoid choking on rage and frustration (and thus lapsing, as does the
Minotaur, into nonlanguage) and on the listener's ability to assemble
sounds into language, to sift noise for its meaning. The oracle advises
him to "follow the cow" (251), and so Cadmus goes from chasing a
butterfly to chasing his lost sister to chasing a hitherto unseen cow,
each chase as futile as the one before it.

Cadmus finds the cow, follows it, and soon attracts a crowd of
people who join him and make him their king. A serpent suddenly
appears and kills all but Cadmus, who, in turn, slays the serpent. The

loss of his companions grieves Cadmus, to whom it seems "as if he were doomed to lose everybody whom he loved, or to see them perish, in one way or another" (258). Cadmus's grief is evocative of the text's stress on sustained loss: lost mother, lost father, drowned sister, lost meaning, lost friends.

Cadmus gains material wealth, but he remains spiritually forlorn. Following the orders of a mysterious voice, he plants the dragon's teeth, from which grow an army of soldiers that battle until only five remain. The voice directs the five to construct a city and make Cadmus their king. At the end of their labors, "a female figure" appears, "wonderfully beautiful, and adorned with a royal robe, and a crown of diamonds over her golden ringlets, and the richest necklace that ever a queen wore" (263). Decked in symbols of wealth and beauty, appearing as suddenly as Europa disappeared long ago, this woman seems to Cadmus to be the end of his search: "His heart thrilled with delight. He fancied it his long-lost sister Europa, now grown to womanhood, coming to make him happy, and to repay him, with her sweet sisterly affection, for all those weary wanderings in quest of her, since he left King Agenor's palace!—for the tears that he had shed, on parting with Phoenix, and Cilix, and Thasus!—for the heart-break that had made the whole world seem dismal to him, over his dear mother's grave!" (263). This litany of Cadmus's suffering encourages the expectation that the sensual, sisterly female is indeed Europa, but this is not so. Loss has led to fruitless searching; fruitless searching has led to dreaming and confusion of reality; dreams and reality now lead to a stranger, "'Harmonia, a daughter of the sky, who is given you instead of sister, and brothers, and friend, and mother. You will find all those dear ones in her alone!'" (264).

Cadmus does achieve spiritual harmony with Harmonia, and thus his quest for Europa (for lost innocence) has resulted in his selfhood. However, the adult reader knows that Harmonia and Cadmus's happy lives together are Hawthorne's construct. In classical mythology the dragon slain by Cadmus was sacred to Mars (McPherson 89), who, in retaliation, caused their daughters and grandchildren to perish. Cadmus's union with Harmonia suggests fulfillment, but the literal and symbolic loss of Europa dominates the text. With permanent loss behind him and the loss of children and grandchildren ahead of him, Cadmus's spiritual harmony at the end of "The Dragon's Teeth" is a temporarily achieved balance, a moment apart from the misery of a loss-filled life.

Yet Cadmus's search for Europa resulted in Europa's becoming much more than a lost young sister. As the object of a lengthy and troubled quest, Europa came to represent an ultimately unachievable solution to all the loss that occurs in life. By expanding Cadmus's sense of reality to include a life that seems half-dreamt, Hawthorne establishes a mode of discourse that enables him, like the pilgrims in "The Dragon's Teeth," to enter an imaginative territory where he can examine the experience of loss. Cadmus's temporary, harmonious balance with the events of his life is a rendering of the imaginative ground that the experience of his quest has allowed him to achieve. For Cadmus and for Hawthorne, process (the process of searching, the process of writing) allows one to come to terms with the losses of one's life, to stand—if only for a moment—in harmony with one's experience.

In "Circe's Palace," Hawthorne disregards Anthon and Homer, his sources for the tale (McPherson 93), and locates Circe, not Ulysses, in the center of the myth. Circe's control of reality and its signs re-create Hawthorne's own neutral territory and personify the conditions that allowed him to write most confidently.

The first danger sign in the tale is a yellow-and-purple bird that approaches Ulysses when he first lands on an unnamed island. Deprived of speech and kingly form by Circe's magic, the bird cannot tell its story. Though Ulysses cannot interpret the bird's chirping, he reads the signs well enough to know that "some danger" awaited him (268).

The bird's presence dissuades Ulysses from exploring the palace he sees in the distance. Returning to the ship, he explains his fears and divides the crew. One group is to be headed by him, the other by Eurylochus; one group is to explore the palace, the other to stay behind and guard the ship. Though all see danger in the exploration of the palace, gluttonous crew members insist on the expedition. After a drawing of shells to determine which group will go, Eurylochus and his crew members set off for the palace.

Again the chirping bird appears, and Eurylochus, like Ulysses, interprets the bird's actions as warnings. His fears are overruled by "the rest of the voyagers, snuffing up the smoke from the palace-kitchen," and by "the most notorious gormandizer in the whole crew," who suggests beginning their meal with the bird itself (272). In Hawthorne's works, such a refusal to read the signs is always a warning that bad things await those who ignore their epistemology.

The next sign of enchantment is "a crystal spring" in which "they beheld their own faces dimly reflected, but so extravagantly distorted by the gush and motion of the water, that each one of them appeared to be laughing at himself and all his companions. So ridiculous were these images of themselves, indeed, that they did really laugh aloud, and could hardly be grave again as soon as they wished" (273–74). These distorted mirror images should warn the crew that something is amiss, that things are more complicated than they seem. Frank Kermode has pointed to Hawthorne's use of mirrors as "mysterious or distorting, denying the possibility of a simple relation between image and reality, between sign and referent" (110). Indeed, Eurylochus senses danger and "felt as if he were walking in a dream" (274), telling his companions, " 'If you take my advice, you will turn back' " (274). Even more strongly in the thrall of "the scent from the palace-kitchen" (274), the voyagers refuse, despite a sudden rush of signs that indicate even more strongly that their reading of the world denies its complexities.

The crew's uncontrolled craving takes them past the "unreal" appearance of the palace, past lions, tigers, and wolves that seem "unreal" in their mildness, and into the palace itself, where Circe's voice distracts them: "With her voice was mingled the noise of a loom, at which she was probably seated, weaving a rich texture of cloth, and intertwining the high and low sweetness of her voice into a rich tissue of harmony" (274, 275, 276). Just as Circe creates the unreality of the palace and the island, creates the fiction that surrounds Eurylochus and his crew, so she creates the fabric she is weaving, the song she is singing, and the events to come. This version of Circe corresponds with the representation of single women, or spin-sters, as "duplicitous witchlike weavers of webs in which to ensnare men (like Circe), metaphysical spinners of Fate (like the Norns), and fictionalizing weavers or plotters of doom" (Gilbert and Gubar 632). Circe has all of the power on the island; she creates the signs, and she controls them.

The crew members, completely enchanted by Circe and her women, are invited "into the inner secrecy of the palace" to a feast where they are seated in "cushioned and canopied thrones" (278, 280). They ignore the aspects of ritual in the occasion, instead conjecturing about food until the narrator interjects: "Ah, the gluttons and gormandizers! You see how it was with them. In the loftiest seats of dignity, on royal thrones, they could think of nothing but their greedy appetite, which was the portion of their nature that they shared with wolves and swine; so that they resembled those vilest of animals far more than they did kings—if, indeed, kings were what they ought to be!" (280). As the crew "swilled down the liquor and gobbled up the food," they "forgot all about their homes, and their wives and children, and all about Ulysses, and everything else, except this banquet at which they wanted to keep feasting forever!" (281–82). The crew members are lost in enchantment, subject to the coarsest elements of their natures and too obsessed to read the signs. Their denial of this world's complexities and their privileging selfishness and greed result in their being turned into swine. In this transformation, they lose the best in their natures and are victim to the worst. Their identities have been appropriated and controlled.

Hawthorne's reading of Circe's transforming the crew ("'Assume your proper shapes, gormandizers, and begone to the sty!'" [282]) is richer than Anthon's but close to that in the edition of Homer that Hawthorne used as his source (McPherson 93). As in Homer, here Circe's actions are understandable and justified (Hawthorne's text has also censured the mariners as "gluttons and gormandizers" resembling the "vilest of animals"). Circe's appearance—"beautiful" and "just as wicked and mischievous as the ugliest serpent that ever was seen" (282)—is, however, Hawthorne's own elaboration. This commingling of beauty and evil is, of course, a traditional representation of powerful women: "Male dread of women, and specifically the infantile dread of maternal autonomy, has historically objectified itself in vilification of women, while male ambivalence about female 'charms' underlies the

traditional images of such terrible sorceress-goddesses as the Sphinx,
Medusa, Circe, Kali, Delilah, and Salome, all of whom possess duplicitous arts that allow them both to seduce and to steal male generative
energy" (Gilbert and Gubar 34). Circe's duplicitous arts are further
shown when she hospitably offers Ulysses wine that, " 'instead of dis-
guising a man, . . . brings him to his true self, and shows him as he
ought to be!' " (290). The wine commands real ("true self") and unreal ("shows him as he ought to be") appearances. It would delight
Circe's niece, Medea, " 'to see me offering this wine to my honored
guest!' " (290). Circe's affectionate invocation of Medea suggests connections of blood, power, and attraction between "charming" women.
Beauty and evil mix in Circe's appearance, behavior (hostess/seduc-
tress), wine, and female associates. Though she is vilified and will be
defeated, she has more power and autonomy than any other person
in the tale. Hawthorne's treatment of her is tantalizingly conventional
and sympathetic.

Eurylochus has told Ulysses that "the marble palace, magnificent as
it looked," is "only a dismal cavern in reality" (284). His description
further defines the female nature of Circe and her art: "A cave is—
as Freud pointed out—a female place, a womb-shaped enclosure, a
house of earth, secret and often sacred" (Gilbert and Gubar 93). Here
Circe's "cavern in reality" is female, secret, and sacred. It is the center
of her power, transcending all other realities.

Ulysses conquers this fortress with help from Quicksilver. He demands that Circe reverse all her transformations or die: "Then drawing
his sword, he seized the enchantress by her beautiful ringlets, and
made a gesture as if he meant to strike off her head at one blow.

" 'Wicked Circe,' cried he, in a terrible voice, 'this sword shall put an
end to thy enchantments! Thou shalt die, vile witch, and do no more
mischief in the world, by tempting human beings into the vices which
make beasts of them!' " (291–92). With the traditional femaleness of
"her beautiful ringlets" in Ulysses' fist and the phallic sword as his
vessel of power, Circe surrenders. Transformations are reversed; Circe
offers " 'true hospitality' "; and all rest in her palace until "refreshed
from the toils and hardships of their voyage" (292, 295).

The depiction of Circe's palace and island as a "dismal cavern in reality" forms an imaginative ground where the boundaries between the actual and the imaginary are permeable from the start. This fictional rendering of a neutral territory where the actual does indeed meet the imaginary—where kings turn into birds, voyagers into swine, and palaces into traps—allows Hawthorne to establish the mode of discourse with which he feels most confident as soon as the tale begins. That discourse frees him to explore the representation of Circe and moves him beyond the common nineteenth-century male artist's view of the beautiful, powerful woman. More powerful than Ulysses (who needs Quicksilver's magic to conquer her), Circe is no Beatrice Rappaccini, whose poisonous nature is a matter of faith, or Georgiana Aylmer, whose female flaw guarantees her humanity. Rather, Circe's power and wickedness are celebrated. Ulysses' condemning tone at sword's point is not Hawthorne's, nor is Circe's fate at sword's point Medusa's. In keeping with the text's ambivalence about Circe, she must be defeated, but she need not—either in traditional myth or in Hawthorne's version of it—be decapitated. Even after her surrender, her power remains intact, her art in a state of flux for the future.

However, this artistically successful and suggestive tale is located in a world of loss: loss of reality, identity, humanity. In this alternative reality, sorrow and misfortune are endemic; all who set foot on the island risk the death of the self. At the same time, this alternative reality of grief and woe is also an imaginative re-creation of Hawthorne's own neutral territory. Successful as it is, then, "Circe's Palace"—the place and the tale—shares the troubled, problematic voices of *Tanglewood Tales*.

In the next story, "The Pomegranate-Seeds," Ceres, "the good lady ... [who] had the care ... of the crops of every kind, all over the earth" (296), and her daughter, Proserpina, are rendered helpless by circumstances, suffer irrevocable loss, and, newly experienced, reshape their lives. Hawthorne's version of the Proserpina-Ceres myth suggests the resonance of losses in his own life. His revision differs significantly from his contemporaries' revisions in its privileging images of confinement and emptiness.[2] His version also differs from Anthon's in its representation of Proserpina as a child, not a goddess (McPherson 100).

Hawthorne's Proserpina is old enough to pick flowers while her mother ripens the harvest and young enough to be disobeying her mother by doing so. As she tugs at the roots of an enchanted shrub, the ground opens and Pluto drives out, snatches her up, and carries her off toward Hades. Neglected by her mother (Ceres is blamed for being away), disobedient, inexperienced (unable to recognize an enchanted shrub when she sees one), and too weak to do more than scream feebly as she is abducted, Proserpina is a victim (had Ceres not been away . . .), a foolish child, and a female in a stereotypical rape scenario (in the arms of a dark, male stranger much larger than she, she screams weakly, drops her flowers, shields her face with her golden hair). Beyond these common images, however, is the central fact that Proserpina's epistemology was inadequate for her circumstances: she could not read the signs, and so she suffers and learns.

Ceres has failed to protect her daughter from this classic case of separation anxiety come to life, fails to hear her daughter's faint cries, and fails to prevent the abduction and violation of her child. The text encourages a view of Ceres as weak and negligent by showing Proserpina's screaming resulting in "many mothers . . . [running] quickly to see if any mischief had befallen their children" (300). In this retelling of the myth, other mothers are alert to their children's potential danger, but Ceres is not. Toward the end of the journey to Hades, Proserpina actually sees Ceres "making the corn grow, and too busy to notice the golden chariot as it went rattling along! The child mustered all her strength, gave one more scream, but was out of sight before Ceres had time to turn her head" (302). Ceres, the representative of organic life, is too busy with the earth's fertility to notice the product of her own fertility. In thriving as earth mother, she has apparently neglected to nurture her own child. As is the case with her daughter, her epistemology is inadequate for her circumstances. Her concern with larger issues of fertility results in her paying the price always envisioned by a punitive culture for the "bad" mother: she loses her child.

Imprisoned in Hades, Proserpina initially clings to the past, refusing Pluto's offers of water from Lethe and refusing to eat or drink. She will not be nurtured without her nurturing mother. She soon adjusts to her enclosure, however, telling Pluto, "'I love you a little'" (324), and declaring that only fruit would tempt her to eat. Once she is given a pomegranate, "dry, old, withered" though it is, the seeds "somehow or other" reach her mouth, "that little red cave" (325). Her own desire in this clearly sexual scene seals her bond with Pluto. The reduction of Proserpina's age is intended to desexualize her and thus to sanitize the myth for children. The element of sexuality, however, has not been sanitized; instead, it has gone underground. The sexual innuendo in the pomegranate scene is coded sexuality located in little red caves and significant seeds. Sexuality is hidden, not eliminated. Like the false endings to "The Minotaur" and "The Pygmies," this is a movement toward denial, not purification. The strategy to desexualize the myth by reducing Proserpina's age fails. The denial of overt sexuality and the lack of a pure world for children remain.

The unappealing condition of the pomegranate offered to Proserpina is the result of Ceres' refusal to nurture the earth while she is unable to nurture her daughter. During Proserpina's stay in Hades, Ceres, like Telephassa in "The Dragon's Teeth," wanders nearly witless searching for her daughter, having abandoned all other work—the work, indeed, that resulted in her absence during her daughter's abduction. The barrenness of mother and earth is emblematic of loss: loss of a loved one, loss of hope, loss of life.

Proserpina is rescued by Quicksilver and returned to her mother, who mourns to learn that Proserpina has put six seeds in her mouth and so is only half-restored to her. Proserpina's cheerfulness contrasts with her mother's grief: Proserpina declares, "'[I] can bear to spend six months in his palace, if he will only let me spend the other six with you'" (329). As the sentence suggests, Pluto now controls Proserpina; he has the power to "let" her spend time with her mother.[3] And Proserpina herself is no longer a baby. Her happiness in the enclosure of Hades reveals her betrayal of her mother and her mother's values. She chooses a life—enclosed, and thus secure; inorganic, and thus barren—that is a kind of death. Her cheerfulness reflects her self-control and newly acquired sense of identity: she is no longer just her mother's child.

The story locates Proserpina's loss of her mother in the moment when, locked in Pluto's arms, she sees her mother and utters her unheard cry for help. Ceres' loss of her daughter is located in the moment when she is reunited with Proserpina and, locked in her daughter's arms, learns of the six seeds and Proserpina's good cheer. Both moments conflate loss with betrayal: Proserpina literally sees her mother as she figuratively sees her mother's inability to save her; Ceres literally sees Proserpina as she figuratively sees her new identity, her adulthood. "The Pomegranate-Seeds" has everything to do with loss: the child's loss of faith in the parent's power, the parent's loss of the child to time, and the grief of both at these inevitabilities, which read so sadly like betrayals.

The final story of *Tanglewood Tales*, "The Golden Fleece," opens with the child Jason inexplicably "sent away from his parents" (330). Thus the story's first sentence suggests the child's loss of and rejection by his parents. Though Jason learns that "his father, King Aeson, had been deprived of the kingdom of Iolcos by a certain Pelias, who would also have killed Jason" had Jason not been sent away (331), that information is given later, allowing the construct of the male child rejected by his parents to dominate.

Jason, grown to manhood, sets out "to punish the wicked Pelias for wronging his dear father, and to cast him down from the throne, and seat himself there instead" (332). Here the son is capable of defeating and displacing the man who defeated his father. Wearing his father's sandals (and thus, like Theseus, following in his father's footsteps), Jason travels to Iolcos, confronts Pelias, and bargains to go "'in quest of the Golden Fleece,'" (340) with Pelias's throne as the prize should he succeed.

To begin his quest, Jason consults the Talking Oak at Dodona. As with the Delphic oracle in "The Dragon's Teeth," the advice at first sounds like the wind, then gradually shapes itself into words: "And now, though it still had the tone of a mighty wind roaring among the branches, it was also like a deep, bass voice, speaking, as distinctly as a tree could be expected to speak" (341). Again, the wisdom of the ages is nearly unreadable and ultimately can tell only the smallest portion of what one needs to know. The tree commands Jason to have a ship built and to have one of its own branches carved into a figurehead for the galley. Jason obeys, and the carver he engages for the task

> found that his hand was guided by some unseen power, and by a skill beyond his own, and that his tools shaped out an image which he had never dreamed of. When the work was finished, it turned out to be the figure of a beautiful woman, with a helmet on her head, from beneath which the long ringlets fell down upon her shoulders. On the left arm was a shield, and in its centre appeared a lifelike representation of the head of Medusa with the snaky locks. The right arm was extended, as if pointing onward. The face of this wonderful statue, though not angry or forbidding, was so grave and majestic, that perhaps you might call it severe; and as for the mouth, it seemed just ready to unclose its lips, and utter words of the deepest wisdom. (342–43)

This "figure of a beautiful woman" is created by man (the bough is harvested by Jason, carved by a male carver) and for man (to guide Jason). The harvesting of the bough, however, has been ordered by a genderless voice, and the carver's hand is guided for him, not by him. The representation of Minerva and the bodiless Medusa that results is therefore not necessarily the creation of man. Though remaining a figurehead, it guides Jason, instructing him in gathering heroes for his crew. This complex depiction of Minerva and Medusa is Hawthorne's addition to the myth (McPherson 104). It joins the women in *Tanglewood Tales* who are gifted with great powers barely held in check by the devices of men (Ariadne's loyalty to her father, Circe's fear of Ulysses' sword, Medea's flight from Aegeus's palace, Ceres' destructive, but not annihilating, response to Proserpina's abduction). Such women seem on the brink of fully asserting their power and controlling the world around them. Their place in Hawthorne's imaginative re-creations of these myths will be discussed later, when the final woman joins these ranks.

Jason sails to meet King Aetes, possessor of the Golden Fleece, who sets two conditions before Jason can try for the prize. First, he must tame two bulls and then use the bulls to "'plough the sacred earth in the grove of Mars, and sow some of the same dragon's teeth from which Cadmus raised a crop of armed men'" (354). In agreeing to Aetes' deadly terms, Jason is one with Theseus and Cadmus, the other kings' sons in *Tanglewood Tales*. Like them, he is both rejected by and superior to his father, and he is the recipient of barely articulated messages from nature. The symbolic representation of the challenge he must meet and defeat invokes both Theseus (the two bulls) and Cadmus (the sowing of the dragon's teeth). This model of the son is thus inscribed in the text. It seems to be a condition of this world that the son must lose the desirable father and confront the evil father. The text appropriates and controls father-son relations and so denies the possibility of relations between father and son outside this model. In *Biographical Stories*, there are contradictions between what Mr. Temple says and what his stories reveal. In *Tanglewood Tales*, there are no such disagreements. Fathers and sons alike are trapped within scripts of loss and rejection.

The child's separation from the parent is further promoted in Medea, King Aetes' daughter, who offers to aid Jason. This is Medea's third appearance in the collection: she is wife to King Aegeus in "The Minotaur," niece to Circe in "Circe's Palace," and here "a beautiful young woman" with "a wonderful intelligence in her face" (354, 355). Jason almost fears Medea, a princess and an enchantress schooled by Circe: if he were "capable of fearing anything, he would have been afraid of making this young princess his enemy; for, beautiful as she now looked, she might, the very next instant, become as terrible as the dragon that kept watch over the Golden Fleece" (355). In the traditional version of this myth, Jason falls in love with Medea and promises her marriage for her help (McPherson 104). In Hawthorne, Jason promises eternal gratitude for which Medea, like Ariadne in "The Minotaur," betrays her father. Ariadne's and Medea's immediate betrayals of their fathers suggest that Theseus and Jason are no more than convenient opportunities for long-awaited treachery. Hawthorne's versions of these myths privilege betrayal instead of love or marriage. Neither Ariadne nor Medea desire love or marriage from these men. Their portrayals (and the way these portrayals differ from the original) promote two conditions of this world: children always betray parents, and powerful women are beautiful and terrible.

In the ensuing scenes, Medea is braver, wiser, and more powerful than Jason. She gives Jason an ointment to protect him from the fiery breath of the bulls, holds his hand as he fearfully approaches the bulls, gives him the dragon's teeth to sow, and instructs him in handling the battle that ensues. Indeed, after Jason has witnessed the deaths of all his soldiers, he says to Medea, " 'To tell you the truth, Princess, the Golden Fleece does not appear so well worth the winning, after what I have here beheld' "; in reply, Medea wisely remarks on the true nature of his quest: " 'True; the Golden Fleece may not be so valuable as you have thought it; but then there is nothing better in the world— and one must needs have an object, you know!' " (362). If one is given to quests—literal or figurative, mental or physical—in a world ruled by rationalism and materialism, then one does indeed need an object. Medea, like Circe, can read the signs of such a world and knows that the value of the quest is the quest itself, not the object at the quest's end. Like the other women in *Tanglewood Tales*, Medea finds her joy in process, not possession.

King Aetes refuses Jason the fleece after hearing that the deeds have been accomplished. When all seems lost, Medea has another plan: "Her black eyes shone upon him with such a keen intelligence, that he felt as if there were a serpent peeping out of them; and, although she had done him so much service, only the night before, he was by no means very certain that she would not do him an equally great mischief, before sunset" (363–64). This representation corresponds with other depictions of women in *Tanglewood Tales*. Male ambivalence about powerful women is revealed in Jason's viewing Medea as duplicitous and inhuman. Medea has determined Jason's actions, and although this has guaranteed his success, it has also made him uncomfortable: he is faced with female autonomy. His suspicions of Medea are not only ungrounded but, worse yet, hypocritical. Though *she* will act honorably toward him throughout the text, *he* will do her "great mischief" by abandoning her. The duplicity is Jason's: he needs to impose a negative reading on Medea and her power precisely because it is female power. He comfortably confronts Pelias's and Aetes' evil power, but

Medea's partakes of an otherness outside phallocentric presumptions. Medea's power as enchantress is Hawthorne's addition to the myth (McPherson 107), a creation that allows the enactment of male dread of powerful women. At the same time, it reveals Jason, holder of such attitudes, to be sometimes fearful, timid, and needy. Hawthorne could therefore identify with these assumptions about male authority yet at the same time (with his portrayal of Jason) distance himself from them. In both cases, the result of this privileging of power relations is that the possibility of true friendship and affection is lost.

Medea leads Jason into the sacred grove at night and, after giving the guarding dragon a sleeping potion, instructs Jason: "'Snatch the prize, and let us begone! You have won the Golden Fleece!'" (367). Despite Medea's use of the first-person plural, this is the last we see and hear of her. Alone, Jason runs to the ship, which immediately sets sail. That Medea tells Jason he has won the fleece is interesting and untrue: Medea has won the Golden Fleece; Jason has been her pawn. Unlike the traditional version of this myth, in which Medea leaves with Jason, Jason here, like the thief and coward he has been in the tale, flees "homeward bound, as if careering along with wings" (368).

It is fitting that Jason flees the scene of "The Golden Fleece" and leaves Medea alone in the grove. Medea, after all, has been the focus throughout much of the tale. Once Minerva and Medusa's head have guided Jason to King Aetes, Medea takes control. She offers her aid to Jason, impresses and frightens him with her power, holds his hand, gives him magic potions, arranges for him to get the Golden Fleece, and, perhaps most important of all, tells him one of the secrets of life, though he does not understand it as such. Her sly commentary on the relative worth of the Golden Fleece ("One must needs have an object, you know!") leaves Jason ample room to question her object, to learn what every woman in *Tanglewood Tales* knows: that dwelling on the object of a quest blinds one and that it is the quest itself, like life itself, that should demand one's attention and command one's best efforts. Ariadne's aid to Theseus, Telephassa's search for Europa, Circe's world of the real and the unreal, Ceres' quest for Proserpina, the Minerva-Medusa figurehead's guidance of Jason, and Medea's aiding of Jason's schemes are all quests that deliver no more than an angry father, a herd of swine, and long days and nights without one's daughter. Yet each quest, each mission, is performed by each woman as carefully and skillfully as any art.

Hawthorne's understanding of this way of reading life is played out in the text of *Tanglewood Tales*. Medea's appearing in different guises in three of the myths stresses her timelessness. She is shown at different points in time and different points in the collection. The complex nature of Medea's characterization shows Hawthorne creating a woman who herself exists as a neutral territory, a place where the actual and the imaginary continually meet. Medea is princess and enchantress, daughter and traitor, friend and foe. Therefore Jason rightly fears that Medea may, in an instant, become as terrible as a dragon. Given Jason's epistemology (parents may vanish, trees may talk), given Medea as a ground where the actual and the imaginary may meet, when Jason is in Medea's presence, his worst dreams may come true (a woman turning into a serpent), even as his fondest wishes are fulfilled. In Medea, Hawthorne voices his admiration for the powerful women in his collection. He constructs Medea herself as a wild card, a living representation of the discourse with which he felt most confident, a discourse that allowed room for the full play of the imagination, a place where the exertions of powerful women could read as brief, well-executed moments of art.

After *Tanglewood Tales* was completed, the Hawthornes sailed for England. Hawthorne would go on to write *The Marble Faun* abroad, and when he returned to America in 1860, he would write essays, edit his notebooks, and attempt another romance, but his writing in America was essentially finished well before he died in 1864.

Written in the confidence of Hawthorne's maturity, *Tanglewood Tales* is a powerful book flooded with themes of loss and creation. In its pages, Hawthorne succeeds—as he had tentatively learned long ago in *Grandfather's Chair*—in establishing that mode of discourse located in the "neutral territory, somewhere between the real world and fairy-land, where the Actual and the Imaginary may meet, and each imbue itself with the nature of the other" (*Scarlet Letter* 36). The timeless nature of classic myths lends itself again, as it did in *A*

Wonder Book, to the full reality of all times and places as Hawthorne approaches his material. Pregnant as the myths are with themes fundamental to the psychological landscape of human nature, they are particularly appropriate for re-creation by Nathaniel Hawthorne.

Hawthorne's understanding of the substance of his re-creation is clearly not a full one. When he wrote the introduction to the collection, he certainly had doubts about the nature of his achievement, doubts that he aired in his thoughts on "Eustace's" completed manuscript:

> Yet, in spite of my experience of his free way of handling them, I did not quite see, I confess, how he could have obviated all the difficulties in the way of rendering them presentable to children. These old legends, so brimming over with everything that is most abhorrent to our Christianized moral-sense—some of them so hideous—others so melancholy and miserable, amid which the Greek Tragedians sought their themes, and moulded them into the sternest forms of grief that ever the world saw;—was such material the stuff that children's playthings should be made of! How were they to be purified? How was the blessed sunshine to be thrown into them? (178–79)

These doubts surface as anxiety about the collection's contents only after the collection has been completed. Hawthorne's need to rewrite the myths as he did was strong enough to stifle these doubts until the last step of his composition, the writing of his introduction. That he did not anticipate or fully recognize the use to which he put the myths is revealed in the coded sexual relationships and the themes of death and loss, which are complicated by lighthearted tones and false happy endings. Caught up as Hawthorne was in the process of rewriting the myths, he could not see the themes that are writ large in *Tanglewood Tales*.

Despite this clouded vision, what Hawthorne invents saves him, as it did in *Biographical Stories*. His use of the classical myths he chooses allows him to enact scenarios and themes of loss and ambiguities of authorship that he could not otherwise express. His re-creations are as problematic as the originals, but, ultimately, he made the myths his own, turned their "melancholy and miserable" themes into themes of his life and his writing. These themes allow his understanding to extend fully beyond the limits of his own transient existence. Like the children who listen to Grandfather's stories in *Famous Old People* and learn lessons of earthly sin and violence, Hawthorne may have found the recent events of his own life impressed upon him his own mortality. Up until this point, Hawthorne had managed to preserve a portion of his innocence, an ability to call up the childlike side of himself and to write it into his fiction, most overtly into his children's books. Provoked by his life's circumstances and his resulting view of the world, Hawthorne loses that essential innocence and moves beyond that once-thriving part of his nature.

Without that ability, things do not resolve themselves happily and credibly in *Tanglewood Tales*; indeed, they rarely resolve themselves at all. The tales that Hawthorne gives birth to in *Tanglewood Tales* are familiars of betrayal, drowning, irresponsibility, and irrevocable, unredeemable loss. No myth in the collection offers us "that lovely and lightsome little figure of Hope" seen in *A Wonder Book*, "What in the world could we do without her?" (*A Wonder Book* 81); in *Tanglewood Tales*, each myth offers a scenario of what in the world *is* done without hope.

No wonder, then, that Hawthorne's introduction ends with a blessing, a cry for a blessing upon himself. In writing out these worlds of loss, Hawthorne gains the strength to continue. I see this point as Hawthorne's turning to full adulthood, the beginning of old age. His seven-year absence from fiction in Liverpool marks his entrance into the world of rationalism and materialism (the world that he had always seen as deathly for the artist) and his exit from the prime of his literary career. The concluding paragraph to *Tanglewood Tales*'s introduction reveals Hawthorne's knowledge that he had been immersed in the world of experience for too long, that his experiences had been too wearying for him to write for children ever again. They will hear no more from him, because he had already gone too far away, much further than Liverpool. Indeed, he will be located in a completely different place—geographically and otherwise—when he writes *The Marble Faun*.

Those who wish to hear the stories that Hawthorne was once able to tell may turn to *Grandfather's Chair*, *Famous Old People*, and *Liberty*

Tree, where the nature of his audience allows him to find a neutral territory as yet unknown to him in his adult fiction; to *Biographical Stories*, where, in frustration, he rejects that happy discourse and tells his truths; to *A Wonder Book*, where he is in the golden age of his art and his life; and, finally, to *Tanglewood Tales*, where he discovers newly probed limits of his childhood audience, newly probed difficulties with recounting thrice-told tales, where he measures what he has lost, finds it to be great indeed, and, in this discovery, airs the inner voices of his depths so that he will not sink under the burden and will be able to continue in the complex culture in which he finds himself. Hawthorne's final call for heaven's blessing on "everybody else, whether grown people or children!" (182), is a heartbreaking blessing that we feel across the years as we look around the sea bobbing with corpses, as we hear the cries of the orphaned children, and as we gaze at the loss-filled faces of our fellow passengers on the voyage through Hawthorne's last reality, the world of *Tanglewood Tales*.

APPENDIX

Historical and Textual Information on the Publication of Hawthorne's Books for Children

For complete historical and textual details concerning Nathaniel Hawthorne's books for children, Roy Harvey Pearce's historical introduction to volume 6 of *The Centenary Edition of the Works of Nathaniel Hawthorne* and Fredson Bowers's two textual introductions in volumes 6 and 7 of the same work are essential reading. Their introductions to the children's books are the most complete accounts of their subjects and have been invaluable to my study.

The first three children's books were each published by Elizabeth Peabody in Boston: *Grandfather's Chair* in December 1840, *Famous Old People* in January 1841, and *Liberty Tree* in March 1841. Peabody also arranged for the reissue of the three books as a collection, published sometime between December 1841 and April 1842, and for the first publication of *Biographical Stories* in April 1842, both by Tappan and Dennet. All four books were reissued the same year in a single collection by Tappan and Dennet titled *Historical Tales for Youth* (all information in this paragraph, Pearce 294).

Hawthorne asked Peabody to be "his go-between in negotiating with the publisher Munroe on the business of reprinting the books and continuing the series" (Pearce 294), but he was prickly about her efforts. On June 23, 1841, he wrote her a formal note, distancing himself from the business of book publishing and telling her to sell the remainder of the first editions of *Grandfather's Chair*, *Famous Old People*, and *Liberty Tree* "on such terms as Miss Peabody thinks best" (*Letters* 15: 547). In February of the following year, still irritated, he wrote formally again on the same subject, referring to himself in third person: "He *now* recommends that they should be got rid of on *any* terms" (*Letters* 15: 609). Peabody's thankless service to Hawthorne had not been small. She had published the books, negotiated with two different publishers for their reissue (unsuccessfully with James Munroe and Company and successfully with Tappan and Dennet), and had been forced to keep the remainder of the first editions herself, advertising *Famous Old People* and *Liberty Tree* for sale at half price (Pearce 295). In 1851, ten years later, she still had at least 250 copies of *Liberty Tree* (*Letters* 15: 610).

The publication and success of *The Scarlet Letter* and *The House of the Seven Gables* freed Hawthorne from unhappy obligations to others in publishing his works. When he described the idea for *A Wonder Book* in an 1851 letter to James Fields, his editor and publisher, Fields responded immediately and enthusiastically. *A Wonder Book* was published by Ticknor, Reed, and Fields on November 8, 1851 (Pearce 305). *Tanglewood Tales* was accepted just as readily and was published in August 1853.

In a letter dated November 27, 1840, days before the publication of *Grandfather's Chair*, Hawthorne asked Sophia to imagine "thy husband, staggering, and puffing, and toiling onward at the gate of the farm, burthened with the unsaleable remnant of Grandfather's Chair. Dear us, what a ponderous, leaden load it will be!" (*Letters* 15: 505). Though Peabody bore the literal burden of the books, Hawthorne saw few profits from *Grandfather's Chair*, *Famous Old People*, *Liberty Tree*, and *Biographical Stories* until 1854. *True Stories from History and Biography* (which included *The Whole History* and *Biographical Stories*) was published in 1851 and 1854. "A total of nine printings—9,000 copies—brought him $667.50 in royalties by 1863" (Pearce 297).

The 1851 printing of *A Wonder Book* resulted in 4,667 copies and $531.00 in royalties. By 1863, the year before his death, Hawthorne had made $1,021.35 on 10,349 copies in print (Pearce 308–9). For *Tanglewood Tales*, Hawthorne had received American royalties of

$771.38 on 6,930 copies and £50 on the British edition (Pearce 309–10). All editions of *True Stories* had retailed at 75¢ (Bowers 6: 325, 328, 330). *A Wonder Book* retailed at 75¢ also (Bowers 7: 373). *Tanglewood Tales* was initially priced at 87½¢ and increased to 88¢ (Bowers 7: 382). By 1863 Hawthorne's books for children had earned him approximately $2,460 in American royalties and £50 in British compensation.

Some publication data from other books of the time may be helpful. *Typee* (1846) earned Herman Melville approximately $2,000 over forty-one years (Howard 298). *The Scarlet Letter*'s (1850) American royalties totaled a little over $1,500 on 7,800 copies in Hawthorne's lifetime (Charvat xvi). Edgar Allan Poe's *Tales* (June 1845) sold 1,500 copies before the year's end and earned Poe $120 in royalties (Tebbel 23). In a few short months in 1852, Harriet Beecher Stowe's *Uncle Tom's Cabin* earned her $10,000 in royalties (Tebbel 55). Fanny Fern's *Fern Leaves from Fanny's Portfolio* (1853) sold 80,000 copies (Douglas 97). Washington Irving had earned $75,000 in royalties from Putnam's (the publisher he chose when he returned from Spain) before he died (Tebbel 38).

Hawthorne's publishing agreements for his children's books as well as his other fictions were competitive with those made by Henry Wadsworth Longfellow, Oliver Wendell Holmes, John Greenleaf Whittier, and other writers of the day (Tebbel 59). Additionally, James Fields was expert at marketing his authors: he used advertisements, reviews, large catalogs, and posters as part of his "genius for promoting authors" (Tebbel 60–61). His reissues of the children's books to capitalize on the success of Hawthorne's novels show him keeping "Hawthorne's name before the public by reprinting his old works and publishing his new ones as fast as they were written. By July, 1852, Fields had seven Hawthorne titles on his list" (Charvat xviii).

Yet Hawthorne never reached a large audience and never had a broad appeal. His use of the Acadian exile in *Famous Old People* is a case in point. After writing on the subject, Hawthorne "had no more interest in it and handed it over to Longfellow, whose book-length poem, published in November 1847, ran to six editions by January and brought the poet approximately $100 a week in royalties during its

boom period" (Mellow 286). Longfellow's gratitude for the subject of
Evangeline ("Still more do I thank you for resigning to me that 'Legend
of Acady!' This success I owe entirely to you" [Longfellow 3: 146])
must have both flattered and frustrated Hawthorne. To have Longfellow in one's professional debt might prove useful, but Hawthorne's
use of the Acadian exile had had all too little success.

The critical reception of the children's books was no less admiring
than that received by his competitors' work and his other fictions.
Evert Duyckinck enthusiastically reviewed *Grandfather's Chair* in the
January 1841 issue of *Arcturus* (Pearce 301). The *Grandfather's Chair*
series (*The Whole History* and then *True Stories*) in the Tappan and
Dennet editions received favorable reviews from *The Pioneer*, *Godey's
Lady's Book and Magazine* (Pearce 296), and the *London Athenaeum*
(Mellow 193). The 1851 reissue of *True Stories* received good reviews
from the *Literary World*, *Harper's Magazine*, and *Graham's Magazine*
(Pearce 296). *A Wonder Book* and *Tanglewood Tales* received enthu-
siastic reviews in both *Graham's Magazine* and *The Literary World*
(Pearce 306).

The picture of Hawthorne's publication success is therefore a complex one. All of his fictions sold, and all did, eventually, make him
money. None of his fictions, however, sold as well as some books by
some of his contemporaries. This lack of large earnings from royalties
should not be confused with a lack of editions. All of his children's
books went into numerous printings. The print runs of *True Stories*,
for instance, began with 2,000 copies printed in 1850 (Bowers 6: 325)
and went to 2,500 copies in 1851 (Bowers 6: 328); the number of copies
printed were 500 in 1854, 500 in 1855, 1,500 in 1856, and 500 each year
in 1857, 1859, 1860, and 1863 (Bowers 6: 330–31). Had Hawthorne's
books been published earlier in his career or had he lived longer, the
royalties would no doubt have been more substantial, though none
would have matched the best-sellers of the day.

The children's books aided his literary career in several ways. They
kept his name before the public in reviews and editions; they added to
his publishers' profits and to his own royalties; and their slow success
kept open the possibility that he could earn money by continuing to
write children's literature. In the end, the children's books enriched

his publishers' lists, his bank account, and his reputation. The sales and editions of the children's books in his lifetime proved that Hawthorne's instincts about juvenile writing—seen in his notebooks, letters, and prefaces to the children's books—were correct: even though writing for children did not make him a fortune (or anything close to one), it was a worthy addition to the literary efforts of a dedicated writer.

NOTES

Introduction

1. John C. Crandall's "Patriotism and Humanitarian Reform in Children's Literature, 1825–1860" is particularly helpful in detailing the emergence of popular juvenile writing. Nationalistic movements against poverty, crime, and slavery and for temperance and peace appeared regularly in children's books and miscellanies of the time.

2. In addition to "Little Annie's Ramble," Hawthorne published two other sentimental children's sketches in this vein: "Little Daffydowndilly" appeared in the *Boys' and Girls' Magazine* in 1843, and "A Good Man's Miracle" appeared in *The Child's Friend* in 1844 (Pearce 288).

3. Arlin Turner's *Hawthorne as Editor* contains selections of the work Hawthorne did for Goodrich while in his employ as editor of *The American Magazine of Useful and Entertaining Knowledge*. Though Hawthorne did not write children's literature for *The American Magazine*, a few sketches in that periodical bear a stylistic resemblance to parts of his later children's books, especially *Grandfather's Chair*. See Turner, *Hawthorne as Editor* (11).

Chapter One. The Transcendence of Temporality: *The Whole History of Grandfather's Chair*

1. After the works of Baym and Colacurcio, the best recent addition to the critical literature on *The Whole History of Grandfather's Chair* has been John W. Crowley's "Hawthorne's New England Epochs." Crowley compares the "coherent historical vision" of *The Whole History* with Hawthorne's later "treatment of the New England present in *The House of the Seven Gables*" (60). Crowley's analysis of *The Whole History* and the connections between the sketches is provocative. In his convincing comparison of *The Whole History* and *The House of the Seven Gables*, he argues that Hawthorne "confined himself to the history of the Chair of State" in *The Whole History* and that "he

probed the 'deeper history' of the family chair," along with "the family house that contains it" (69), in *The House of the Seven Gables*.

2. The sentimental pieties of the Victorian treatment of little girls result in more attention being paid to "little Alice" than to her older sister, Clara. The portrayal of Emily in *Biographical Stories* will be similarly sketchy. Clara's and Emily's roles are limited to a brief introduction and then a line or two of general description later in the text. The male children consistently receive greater authorial attention than their female counterparts, unless the female is the prototype for untainted innocence, as is Alice. Hawthorne's preference for that innocence in children, male or female, is apparent in the introduction to *Tanglewood Tales*, where he woefully describes how his young auditors from *A Wonder Book* have grown to the point where they have even learned to read and write. The acquisition of such skills can lead only to knowledge, experience, and adulthood.

Chapter Two. The Denial of Invention: *Biographical Stories for Children*

1. Laura B. Kennelly suggests connections between Hawthorne's historical treatment of British history in "Young Goodman Brown" and *Biographical Stories*.

2. John Idol usefully discusses biographical details in the sketch of Benjamin West.

3. Hawthorne's writing of *Biographical Stories* is so underdeveloped that his intentions, as well as Edward's understanding, are called into question here. The text encourages such problems with intentionality. Unlike the other children's books, sections of *Biographical Stories* are so loosely connected as to seem almost random. Though these moments interfere with the text, they also reinforce Hawthorne's connection to Edward and stress the ambiguity of the actions and reactions of author and auditor.

4. The corresponding male portraits in *Biographical Stories* are notable for the absence of women. Femininity plays no role in the earlier portraits of Dr. Johnson, Benjamin West, Isaac Newton, Oliver Cromwell, and Benjamin Franklin. Mothers or mother figures are rarely mentioned; wives are not mentioned at all; and no woman plays any role, major or minor, in Hawthorne's telling of the other biographical stories. The relation of father with son or, for Oliver Cromwell, uncle with son consumes Hawthorne's attention in the earlier stories. The guidance given by the fathers in the stories consistently results in their sons' achievement later in life.

This steady stream of masculinity is deformed once Hawthorne reaches Christina and Gustavus. Gustavus's masculinity—the masculinity that shapes Christina—is presented as misguided, defiant, inappropriate, and a clear violation of cultural and almost religious restrictions ("Providence had created her to be a woman, and that it was not for him to make a man of her" [277]). Christina's masculinity (her identification with her father, separation from her mother, physical appearance, and putative denial of her own sex) is also a deformed version of male responses to fathers in earlier stories. Christina responds to her father as do the other children in *Biographical Stories*. That Hawthorne chose to negatively highlight Gustavus's and Christina's masculinity helps to reveal his own recoiling from overt masculinity in his art and life.

5. Christina's appearance is at odds with the nineteenth-century view of children, with which Hawthorne was clearly familiar. Hawthorne's portrayals of children throughout his fiction correspond closely to nineteenth-century ideals of cherubic, flowerlike children. The child auditors featured in the frame tales of *The Whole History of Grandfather's Chair*, *Biographical Stories*, and *A Wonder Book* fit this mold without exception. Hawthorne's inclination toward sentimentalism of childhood reaches its peak in *A Wonder Book*, where all the children have flower names (Primrose, Periwinkle, Sweet Fern, and Dandelion, for instance) that emphasize their decorative roles as listeners and their innocent, natural condition.

Mary Lynn Stevens Heininger, in her essay "Children, Childhood, and Change in America, 1820–1920," discusses the progression of the sentimentalism of the image of childhood: "First in portraiture and illustration during the mid-1850s, and later in three-dimensional household accessories, a formulaic picture of children began to emerge. Perhaps with their roots in portrayals of Renaissance cherubs, these images depicted children as wide-eyed [and] chubby-cheeked" (23). Once these cherubic children reached "school age," the male children "disappeared from these images" and gave way to "the stereotype of the wily, dirty-faced lad . . . [and] the image of the docile and immaculate little girl" (26). Nineteenth-century narratives for girls reinforce the general importance of an attractive physical appearance. Christina's plainness violates the depiction of children that nineteenth-century Americans found necessary to their view of themselves and their world. For Hawthorne, Christina's historically recorded plainness would classify her as an atypical child.

Christina's appearance at birth seems to have been noted in virtually all records of Gustavus's reign. Christina herself almost cheerfully corroborates this description, remarking, in her autobiography, that the classification of her as "a girl and ugly . . . wasn't far wrong because I was as dark as a little Moor" (qtd. in Masson 21). There is no reason to suspect that Christina's autobiography was Hawthorne's source of information, however. Walter Harte's *History of the Life of Gustavus Adolphus, King of Sweden* is a much more likely candidate. A copy of Harte's book was twice withdrawn from the Salem Athenaeum in Hawthorne's name in 1827 (Kesselring 53). Hawthorne was no longer living in Salem in 1841, when he was writing *Biographical Stories*, and any record of his having consulted Harte's book during that time has not been recovered. The skeletal information in Hawthorne's "Queen Christina" is close enough to the information in Harte's book (which subscribes to commonly held views of Christina as both plain and eccentric) to render it likely that it was Hawthorne's source.

6. Christina's relationship with her mother was actually more complicated than Hawthorne probably knew. Georgina Masson, in her biography of Christina, recounts that midwives at Christina's birth, "buoyed up by the predictions of astrologers, . . . believed her to be a boy, . . . since Christina was born with a caul which enveloped her from her head to her knees, leaving only her face, arms and lower part of her legs free; moreover she was covered with hair" (20–21). Maria Elenora, Christina's mother, "was in no condition to be told the truth and they waited several days before breaking the news to her" (21).

7. The juxtaposition of first-person narrator Miles Coverdale and his attraction for and description of the darkly beautiful Zenobia in *The Blithedale Romance* (1852) mimic to some extent the roles of Mr. Temple and Christina. Zenobia is presented as a powerful, strong, queenlike woman of untraditional beauty. The story of her life and death is explored, related, and judged by Miles Coverdale, dilettante writer. Coverdale's authority is undercut from virtually the beginning of the book, and Hawthorne differentiates so clearly between himself and his narrator that there is little chance for the reader to invest the character Coverdale with Hawthorne's authority.

Chapter Three.   The Renewal of Imagination and Faith: *A Wonder Book for Boys and Girls*

1. Elizabeth Peck cogently argues for the nonsexist nature of the audience in *A Wonder Book*'s frame stories. Peck notes Hawthorne's use of plural referents, insistence on the children as a collective unit, and floral names as rhetorical strategies for avoiding gender-specific language. The children's

energetic activities are seen as similarly nonsexist: girls and boys alike rough-house, picnic, and pick flowers. Peck is less convincing in her discussion of Eustace's role as only incidentally male.

2. I would argue that it is Medusa, not Perseus, who permanently defeats King Polydectes and his subjects, reducing them to images without sight. In death and dismemberment, she can accomplish what Danae cannot even approach in life and health. Medusa, as the distorted mirror image of Danae, is in life an articulate, powerful, feared woman. She is therefore both monstrous and the dark double of Danae. In slaying her, Perseus slays the female power that would have allowed his mother to do more than cower helplessly in the protection of the temple. By that same sword's stroke, he preserves his own power as narrator, able both to slay a woman whose existence is a rejection of submissive silence and to protect a woman whose existence is so silent that she is never seen or heard in "The Gorgon's Head."

Chapter Four. The Loss of Hope: *Tanglewood Tales*

1. Even a cursory reading of *Tanglewood Tales* will reveal the irony in Haw-thorne's satisfaction with the collection and his classification of them as "old baby stories." Hawthorne's inability (unwillingness?) to negotiate the tales' content is clear in this naming, as is his ambivalence about their content. See Nina Baym's *Shape of Hawthorne's Career* (212–15) for a discussion of the sexual relationships hidden in *Tanglewood Tales.*

2. In *Margaret and Her Friends*, the Proserpina-Ceres myth is discussed by Margaret Fuller, Ralph Waldo Emerson, Elizabeth Peabody, George Ripley, William Story, and others. At first, the discussion seems to provide a dis-course that also sees loss and betrayal in the myth: "The pilgrimages of the more prominent of these goddesses, Ceres and Isis, seem to indicate the life which loses what is dear in childhood, to seek in weary pain for what after all can be but half regained. . . . This era in Mythology seems to mark the progress from an unconscious to a conscious state. Persephone's periodical exile shows the impossibility of resuming an unconsciousness from which we have been once aroused, the need thought has, having once felt the influence of the Seasons, to retire into itself" (519). The discussion moves from loss to Proserpina's new consciousness and thus (in a typically transcendentalist movement) her individuality, her awareness. Proserpina's six months in Hades are read as a painful victory for growth, thought, and consciousness. The separation of mother and daughter *as* mother and daughter in Hawthorne's "The Pomegranate-Seeds" is absent, as is Pluto's control over Proserpina, the

enclosure that is Hades, and the barren state of Ceres and the earth. Fuller and her conversationalists see Proserpina's time in Hades as a necessary exile in which to fulfill a need of the inner, divine self. Hawthorne carefully distinguishes between Pluto's "letting" Proserpina stay on earth periodically and Proserpina's willing acquiescence to Pluto's desire for her to remain in Hades the rest of the time. For Hawthorne, if Proserpina is asserting her individualism, she is doing so only in confinement, only because Pluto "lets" her do so. Where Fuller and friends privilege the resulting consciousness in the action of the myth, Hawthorne privileges the resulting confinement and emptiness.

3. Proserpina's happiness and Hawthorne's unwillingness to negotiate the events that have led up to it (and the restrictions that must follow) are further suggested in the giddy, adolescent rush of language with which Proserpina responds to her mother's mourning (and which ends the story, effectively cutting off any response by Ceres or any intrusion of mournful facts): " 'Do not speak so harshly of poor King Pluto,' said Proserpina, kissing her mother. 'He has some very good qualities. . . . He certainly did very wrong to carry me off; but then, as he says, it was but a dismal sort of life for him, to live in that great, gloomy place, all alone; and it has made a wonderful change in his spirits, to have a little girl to run up stairs and down. There is some comfort in making him so happy; and so, upon the whole, dearest mother, let us be thankful that he is not to keep me the whole year round!' " (329).

 WORKS CITED

Anthon, Charles. *A Classical Dictionary*. New York: Harper and Brothers, 1848.

Auerbach, Nina. *Woman and the Demon: The Life of a Victorian Myth*. Cambridge: Harvard UP, 1982.

Baym, Nina. "Hawthorne's Myths for Children: The Author versus His Audience." *Studies in Short Fiction* 10 (1973): 35–46.

———. *The Shape of Hawthorne's Career*. Ithaca: Cornell UP, 1976.

Bell, Michael Davitt. *Hawthorne and the Historical Romance of New England*. Princeton: Princeton UP, 1971.

Bettelheim, Bruno. *The Uses of Enchantment: The Meaning and Importance of Fairy Tales*. New York: Knopf, 1976.

Billman, Carol. "Nathaniel Hawthorne: 'Revolutionizer' of Children's Literature." *Studies in American Fiction* 10 (Spring 1982): 107–14.

Bowers, Fredson. Textual Introduction. *True Stories from History and Biography*. By Nathaniel Hawthorne. Columbus: Ohio State UP, 1972. 313–36. Vol. 6 of *The Centenary Edition of the Works of Nathaniel Hawthorne*. 20 vols. to date. Ed. William Charvat, Roy Harvey Pearce, Claude M. Simpson. 1962–.

———. Textual Introduction. *A Wonder Book and Tanglewood Tales*. By Nathaniel Hawthorne. Columbus: Ohio State UP, 1972. 371–89. Vol. 7 of *The Centenary Edition of the Works of Nathaniel Hawthorne*. 20 vols. to date. Ed. William Charvat, Roy Harvey Pearce, Claude M. Simpson. 1962–.

Bridge, Horatio. *Personal Recollections of Nathaniel Hawthorne*. New York: Harper and Brothers, 1893.

Charvat, William. Introduction. *The Scarlet Letter*. By Nathaniel Hawthorne. Columbus: Ohio State UP, 1962. xv–xxviii. Vol. 1 of *The Centenary Edition of the Works of Nathaniel Hawthorne*. 20 vols. to date. Ed. William Charvat, Roy Harvey Pearce, Claude M. Simpson. 1962–.

Christina, Queen of Sweden. *The Works of Christina, Queen of Sweden*. London: Wilson and Durham, 1753.

Colacurcio, Michael. *The Province of Piety: Moral History in Hawthorne's Early Tales*. Cambridge: Harvard UP, 1984.

Collingwood, R. G. *The Idea of History*. Oxford: Oxford UP, 1962.

Cott, Jonathan. *Pipers at the Gates of Dawn*. New York: Random House, 1983.

Crandall, John C. "Patriotism and Humanitarian Reform in Children's Literature, 1825–1860." *American Quarterly* 21 (1969): 3–22.

Crews, Frederick. *The Sins of the Fathers*. New York: Oxford UP, 1966.

Crowley, John W. "Hawthorne's New England Epochs." *ESQ* 25 (2nd Quarter 1979): 62–70.

Dauber, Kenneth. *Rediscovering Hawthorne*. Princeton: Princeton UP, 1977.

Douglas, Ann. *The Feminization of American Culture*. New York: Knopf, 1977.

Erlich, Gloria C. *Family Themes and Hawthorne's Fiction*. New Brunswick: Rutgers UP, 1984.

Fiedler, Leslie A. *Love and Death in the American Novel*. New York: Stein and Day, 1966.

Fuller, Margaret. Selection from "Margaret and Her Friends." *The Rise of Modern Mythology, 1680–1860*. Ed. Burton Feldman and Robert D. Richardson. Bloomington: Indiana UP, 1972. 519–23.

Gilbert, Sandra M., and Susan Gubar. *The Madwoman in the Attic*. New Haven: Yale UP, 1984.

Harte, Walter. *The History of the Life of Gustavus Adolphus, King of Sweden*. London: n.p., 1767.

Hawthorne, Julian. *Nathaniel Hawthorne and His Wife*. Boston: Houghton Mifflin, 1895.

Hawthorne, Nathaniel. *The American Notebooks*. Columbus: Ohio State UP, 1972. Vol. 8 of *The Centenary Edition of the Works of Nathaniel Hawthorne*. 20 vols. to date. Ed. William Charvat, Roy Harvey Pearce, Claude M. Simpson. 1962–.

————. *Biographical Stories for Children*. True Stories from History and Biography. Columbus: Ohio State UP, 1972. 211–84. Vol. 6 of *The Centenary Edition of the Works of Nathaniel Hawthorne*. 20 vols. to date. Ed. William Charvat, Roy Harvey Pearce, Claude M. Simpson. 1962–.

————. *Famous Old People*. True Stories from History and Biography. Columbus: Ohio State UP, 1972. 70–139. Vol. 6 of *The Centenary Edition of the Works of Nathaniel Hawthorne*. 20 vols. to date. Ed. William Charvat, Roy Harvey Pearce, Claude M. Simpson. 1962–.

————. *Grandfather's Chair*. True Stories from History and Biography. Columbus: Ohio State UP, 1972. 7–67. Vol. 6 of *The Centenary Edition of the Works of Nathaniel Hawthorne.* 20 vols. to date. Ed. William Charvat, Roy Harvey Pearce, Claude M. Simpson. 1962–.

——. *The Letters, 1813–1843.* Columbus: Ohio State UP, 1984. Vol. 15 of *The Centenary Edition of the Works of Nathaniel Hawthorne.* 20 vols. to date. Ed. William Charvat, Roy Harvey Pearce, Claude M. Simpson, Thomas Woodson. 1962–.

——. *The Letters, 1843–1853.* Columbus: Ohio State UP, 1985. Vol. 16 of *The Centenary Edition of the Works of Nathaniel Hawthorne.* 20 vols. to date. Ed. William Charvat, Roy Harvey Pearce, Claude M. Simpson, Thomas Woodson. 1962–.

——. *Liberty Tree. True Stories from History and Biography.* Columbus: Ohio State UP, 1972. 141–210. Vol. 6 of *The Centenary Edition of the Works of Nathaniel Hawthorne.* 20 vols. to date. Ed. William Charvat, Roy Harvey Pearce, Claude M. Simpson. 1962–.

——. *The Scarlet Letter.* Columbus: Ohio State UP, 1972. Vol. 1 of *The Centenary Edition of the Works of Nathaniel Hawthorne.* 20 vols. to date. Ed. William Charvat, Roy Harvey Pearce, Claude M. Simpson. 1962–.

——. *Tanglewood Tales. A Wonder Book and Tanglewood Tales.* Columbus: Ohio State UP, 1972. 173–368. Vol. 7 of *The Centenary Edition of the Works of Nathaniel Hawthorne.* 20 vols. to date. Ed. William Charvat, Roy Harvey Pearce, Claude M. Simpson. 1962–.

——. *True Stories from History and Biography.* Columbus: Ohio State UP, 1972. Vol. 6 of *The Centenary Edition of the Works of Nathaniel Hawthorne.* 20 vols. to date. Ed. William Charvat, Roy Harvey Pearce, Claude M. Simpson. 1962–.

——. *Twice-Told Tales.* Columbus: Ohio State UP, 1974. Vol. 9 of *The Centenary Edition of the Works of Nathaniel Hawthorne.* 20 vols. to date. Ed. William Charvat, Roy Harvey Pearce, Claude M. Simpson. 1962–.

——. *A Wonder Book for Boys and Girls. A Wonder Book and Tanglewood Tales.* Columbus: Ohio State UP, 1972. 1–171. Vol. 7 of *The Centenary Edition of the Works of Nathaniel Hawthorne.* 20 vols. to date. Ed. William Charvat, Roy Harvey Pearce, Claude M. Simpson. 1962–.

Hedges, William L. *Washington Irving, 1802–1832.* Baltimore: Johns Hopkins UP, 1965.

Heininger, Mary Lynn Stevens. "Children, Childhood, and Change in America, 1820–1920." *A Century of Childhood, 1820–1920.* Ed. Mary Lynn Stevens Heininger. 1–32. Rochester: Margaret Woodbury Strong Museum, 1984.

Hoffman, Daniel. "Myth, Romance, and the Childhood of Man." *Hawthorne*

Centenary Essays. Ed. Roy Harvey Pearce. Columbus: Ohio State UP, 1964. 197–219.

Howard, Leon. Historical Note. *Typee*. By Herman Melville. Ed. Harrison Hayford, Hershel Parker, G. Thomas Tanselle. Evanston and Chicago: Northwestern UP and Newberry Library, 1968. 277–302. Vol. 1 of *The Northwestern-Newberry Edition of the Writings of Herman Melville*. 8 vols. to date. 1968–.

Hutner, Gordon. *Secrets and Sympathy: Forms of Disclosure in Hawthorne's Novels*. Athens: U of Georgia P, 1988.

Idol, John. "Hawthorne's Biographical Sketch of Benjamin West." *Artes Liberales* 7 (Spring 1981): 1–7.

Kennelly, Laura B. "Hawthorne and Goldsmith?: British History in 'Young Goodman Brown' and *Biographical Stories*." *Journal of American Studies* 23 (August 1989): 295–97.

Kermode, Frank. *The Classic: Literary Images of Permanence and Change*. New York: Viking Press, 1975.

Kesselring, Marion. *Hawthorne's Reading, 1828–1850*. Folcroft, Pa.: Folcroft Library Editions, 1975.

Longfellow, Henry Wadsworth. *The Letters of Henry Wadsworth Longfellow*. Ed. Andrew Hilen. Vol. 3. Cambridge: Harvard UP, 1972. 6 vols. 1966–82.

Lurie, Alison. *Don't Tell the Grown-Ups: Subversive Children's Literature*. Boston: Little, Brown, 1990.

Masson, Georgina. *Queen Christina*. New York: Farrar, Straus, and Giroux, 1969.

McPherson, Hugo. *Hawthorne as Myth-Maker*. Toronto: U of Toronto P, 1969.

Mellow, James R. *Nathaniel Hawthorne in His Times*. Boston: Houghton Mifflin, 1980.

Miller, Edwin Haviland. *Melville*. New York: Braziller, 1975.

Murray, Peter B. "Mythopoesis in *The Blithedale Romance*." *PMLA* 75 (December 1960): 591–96.

Pearce, Roy Harvey. Historical Introduction. *True Stories from History and Biography*. By Nathaniel Hawthorne. Ed. William Charvat, Roy Harvey Pearce, Claude M. Simpson. Columbus: Ohio State UP, 1972. 287–311. Vol. 6 of *The Centenary Edition of the Works of Nathaniel Hawthorne*. 20 vols. to date. 1962–.

Peck, Elizabeth. "Hawthorne's Nonsexist Narrative Framework: The Real Wonder of *A Wonder Book*." *Children's Literature Association Quarterly* 10 (Fall 1985): 116–19.

Praz, Mario. *The Romantic Agony*. New York: Oxford UP, 1966.

Sale, Roger. *Fairy Tales and After.* Cambridge: Harvard UP, 1978.

Schorer, Calvin Earl. "The Juvenile Literature of Nathaniel Hawthorne." Diss. U of Chicago, 1949.

Sealts, Merton M. *Melville's Reading.* Madison: U of Wisconsin P, 1966.

Struwwelpeter. Frankfort on the Main: Literarische Anstalt, n.d.

Sundquist, Eric. *Home as Found.* Baltimore: Johns Hopkins UP, 1979.

Tanner, Tony. *The Reign of Wonder.* Cambridge: Cambridge UP, 1965.

Tebbel, John. *Between Covers: The Rise and Transformation of American Book Publishing.* New York: Oxford UP, 1987.

Tompkins, Jane. *Sensational Designs: The Cultural Work of American Fiction, 1790–1860.* New York: Oxford UP, 1985.

Tryon, W. S., and William Charvat, eds. *The Cost Books of Ticknor and Fields, 1832–1858.* New York: Bibliographical Society of America, 1949.

Turner, Arlin. *Hawthorne as Editor: Selections from His Writing in "The American Magazine of Useful and Entertaining Knowledge."* Baton Rouge: Louisiana State UP, 1941.

———. *Nathaniel Hawthorne: A Biography.* New York: Oxford UP, 1980.

Warren, Joyce W. *The American Narcissus: Individualism and Women in Nineteenth-Century American Fiction.* New Brunswick: Rutgers UP, 1984.

INDEX